What About?
Golden Retrievers

Dan Rice, DVM

HOWELL
BOOK
HOUSE

Contents

1 What Exactly Is a Golden Retriever?   1

2 How Does a Golden Retriever Behave?   16

3 How Will My Golden Retriever Grow
and Develop?   33

4 How Healthy Are Golden Retrievers?   45

5 What Should My Golden Retriever Eat?   63

6 How Do I Groom a Golden Retriever?   78

7 What's Involved in Training a Golden Retriever?   89

8 What Kind of Exercise Does a Golden Retriever
Need?   106

9 Where Should I Get My Golden Retriever?   119

10 How Do I Register My Golden Retriever?   135

How Can I Learn More?   144

Index   148

1 What Exactly Is a Golden Retriever?   1

What exactly is a Golden Retriever?

What are Golden Retrievers used for?

Why does my Golden love to swim?

How big do Goldens get?

How active are Goldens?

Are Goldens good watchdogs?

Do Goldens shed a lot?

What does a Golden need from me?

Why are Goldens so popular?

How long do Goldens live?

How long do Goldens stay puppies?

Why is there so much difference between a Golden show dog and a Golden pet?

Is there a difference between hunting Goldens and pet Goldens?

What are the top 10 reasons people want a Golden Retriever for a pet?

What are the top 10 reasons people give up their Golden Retriever after they've acquired one?

What kinds of people will best be able to develop a Golden into a good pet?

What kinds of people will probably have difficulty managing a Golden Retriever as a pet?

Why shouldn't I want a Golden?

2 How Does a Golden Retriever Behave?   16

How do adult Golden Retrievers behave as pets?

What is typical Golden puppy behavior?

What is *acceptable* Golden behavior?

What is a Golden's attitude toward being a house dog and family pet?

How are Goldens with children?

How are Goldens with older people?

How are Goldens with people who aren't members of the family?

How are Goldens with other family pets?

Are Goldens aggressive toward other dogs?

Are Goldens aggressive with people?

Are there special behavior problems particular to Goldens?

What is the general temperament of Goldens?

Can my Golden live outdoors?

Can I safely leave my Golden home alone while I'm at work?

3   **How Will My Golden Retriever Grow and Develop?**   **33**

What's unique about a Golden Retriever's physical development?

What's unique about a Golden Retriever's mental development?

How much canine socialization does a Golden puppy need?

How much human socialization does a Golden puppy need?

What can I expect from a developing young adult Golden?

Are adult Goldens always predictable?

At what age should I consider my Golden a senior citizen?

4   **How Healthy Are Golden Retrievers?**   **45**

How healthy are Goldens in general?

What do genetics have to do with a Golden's health?

What are some hereditary conditions that affect Golden Retrievers?

How common are allergies in Goldens?

How much will it cost per year to keep my Golden healthy?

How do I find a good veterinarian?

What vaccinations does my Golden need?

Do I have to spay or neuter my Golden?

What if I want my female Golden to have puppies or my male to be a father?

Do all dogs have worms?

Do I need to worry about fleas and ticks?

Why does my Golden scratch her ears all the time?

Why is my old Golden losing her hair on each hip and on her elbows?

What is heatstroke?

5   What Should My Golden Retriever Eat?   63

Why is my Golden's diet important?

What kind of diet does a Golden need to be healthy?

Do all adult Goldens have the same nutritional requirements?

Are puppies' nutritional needs different?

Do seniors need a different diet?

What are all those special diets I see at the vet's office?

Which dog food should I buy?

Aren't all dog foods pretty much alike?

How do I interpret dog food labels?

How often should I feed my Golden?

Are Goldens big eaters?

Can I feed my Golden treats?

Can I feed my Golden table scraps?

Should I give my Golden leftover steak bones?

6   How Do I Groom a Golden Retriever?   78

What does grooming a Golden entail?

Why is grooming important?

What are the special characteristics of a Golden's coat?

What equipment do I need for grooming?

How much brushing and combing does my Golden need?

Do Goldens shed seasonally?

Does my Golden's hair need to be trimmed?

What are mats?

How often does my Golden need a bath?

Do I need to trim my Golden's nails?

Does a Golden need special ear care?

What if he has gunk in his eyes?

What are grass awns?

What are hotspots?

What about dental care?

Do anal sacs cause a problem in Goldens?

What are calluses?

7   What's Involved in Training a Golden Retriever?   89

How easy is it to train a Golden Retriever?

What is *trainability*?

Why is it important to train my Golden?

What training does my Golden need to be a well-behaved pet?

How much time will I have to spend training my Golden
Retriever?

What will happen to my Golden's behavior if I don't have time to
train him regularly?

Do I need to hire a professional trainer?

Do I need to join a training class?

What is special about training a Golden?

What principles should I remember when I begin training my dog?

What is dominance training?

What is compulsion training?

What equipment do I need to train my Golden?

What about crates and ex-pens?

What's the best way to housebreak my Golden pup?

What is the Canine Good Citizen program?

Can I train my Golden to assist me with a disability?

What are therapy dogs?

**8   What Kind of Exercise Does a Golden Retriever
      Need?**   **106**

Do Golden Retrievers generally require a lot of exercise?

How much exercise does a Golden puppy need?

At what stage can I exercise my puppy outside the yard?

How much exercise should a young adult get?

How does exercise affect my Golden's physical development?

Does a senior Golden require much exercise?

What can happen if my Golden doesn't get the exercise she
needs?

Can I let my dog run free during the day?

What if I don't have a fenced-in yard?

What's the best backyard exercise for a dog?

How can I exercise my Golden without a fenced yard?

How do I exercise my Golden's mind?

What if I want to get involved in tracking trials?

What about hunting with my dog?

What other canine sports can my Golden and I can participate in?

9   Where Should I Get My Golden Retriever?   **119**

Am I truly ready for a new puppy?

Should I buy my spouse a surprise puppy?

What is the best time of year to get a Golden?

Do I want a male or female?

Would I be happier with an older dog?

Is it easy to obtain a Golden Retriever?

What is a responsible breeder?

How do I find such a breeder?

What can I expect the breeder to ask me?

What do I need to ask the breeder?

What is a show-quality puppy?

What is a pet-quality puppy?

What is meant by form and function?

How soon can I take home my puppy?

What about the Internet or a pet shop?

Where do the puppies in pet shops come from?

Can I trust newspaper ads to find a good Golden pup?

I feel sorry for this sick puppy. Can I take him home and nurse him back to health?

What is Golden Retriever rescue?

Can a rescued Golden make a good pet?

10 How Do I Register My Golden Retriever?   **135**

What does it mean when a dog is registered?

What does registration guarantee?

What is the AKC?

What are a dog's *papers* and what do they cost?

What other registries are doing business in the United States?

What is a pedigree?

What is a title?

What about health guarantees?

Is there an average Golden Retriever price?

What contributes to the price of a Golden Retriever puppy?

How Can I Learn More?   **144**

Golden Retriever Clubs

Purebred Dog Clubs

Hunting Dog Clubs

Activity Organizations

Health Organizations

Service Organizations

Pet Loss Hotlines

Books

Index   **148**

1

What Exactly Is a Golden Retriever?

What exactly is a Golden Retriever? • What are Golden Retrievers used for? • Why does my Golden love to swim? • How big do Goldens get? • How active are Goldens? • Are Goldens good watchdogs? • Do Goldens shed a lot? • What does a Golden need from me? • Why are Goldens so popular? • How long do Goldens live? • How long do Goldens stay puppies? • Why is there so much difference between a Golden show dog and a Golden pet? • Is there a difference between hunting Goldens and pet Goldens? • What are the top 10 reasons people want a Golden Retriever for a pet? • What are the top 10 reasons people give up their Golden Retriever after they've acquired one? • What kinds of people will best be able to develop a Golden into a good pet? • What kinds of people will probably have difficulty managing a Golden Retriever as a pet? • Why shouldn't I want a Golden?

What exactly is a Golden Retriever?

It's a medium-size sporting dog, weighing between 55 and 75 pounds, although either sex may be slightly smaller or larger than the standard. A Golden's coat is thick and wavy but never curly, of medium length, and is solid colored in any shade of gold. A typical Golden is a happy character who dotes on his family and likes other dogs.

What are Golden Retrievers used for?

Sportsmen originally bred Golden Retrievers to retrieve waterfowl and upland game birds. The hunter shot the bird, and then it was the dog's job to bring the bird to the hunter's hand, retrieving it from water, dense underbrush or wherever the bird happened to land. Good retrievers picked each bird up gently and brought it back intact. The dogs hunted under trainers and professional handlers, and many are still used for those purposes.

Today's Golden is more often kept as a pet and family companion. He's strong and powerful, has a moderately high energy level and can play, work or swim for many hours in almost any weather. Goldens are highly trainable and active in canine sports, and they excel in obedience trials; agility and fly ball contests; Frisbee competitions; and more recently, in synchronized freestyle dancing exhibitions. They are superb companions for hikers, bikers, and backpackers.

Considering the Golden's heritage, it's little wonder that trained Goldens often compete in tracking and scenting contests and are valuable as drug, contraband, and munitions sniffers. The practical scenting skills needed following disasters and avalanches are within the realm of possibility for the sensitive nose of the Golden.

Goldens are superior guide dogs for the blind, and many are used as therapy dogs who bring their cheerful wagging tails and earnest expressions to long-term care facilities and hospital patients. Goldens often are trained as assistance dogs for the handicapped, and are large enough to fetch and carry sizable objects to wheelchair-bound owners. Specially trained Goldens nudge their hearing-impaired owners when the doorbell, telephone or alarm bell rings.

Just how versatile is a Golden?

Versatility is the Golden's strongest suit. Part of this flexibility is associated with his even temperament, and more is due to his penchant to please his human companions. His cleverness and intelligence serve him well in every pursuit. His trainability and willingness to bond with families rather than specific individuals are also part of the Golden's versatility.

What's a dual-purpose dog?

It's one who has two separate but nearly equal purposes for its existence. For example, a Golden might be proficient in tracking trials and also be a gundog or retriever trial competitor, or a combination obedience dog and gundog or show dog. Goldens have so many diverse uses that nearly every one is at least a dual-purpose dog.

Where do retrievers come from?

During the 1920s Goldens came to the United States from Great Britain. Retrievers of every description have come from all over Europe and parts of Asia. Probably they were developed from companion dogs who showed a propensity for chasing wounded birds, catching them and bringing them to their handlers. Spaniels, waterfowl retrievers and upland game bird dogs all have individual physical characteristics and histories.

Why, when and where did Golden Retrievers originate?

There's a great but probably fictitious story about the Golden's origin that's worth repeating. According to an ancient report that's still accepted by some authorities (and discounted by most), the Golden Retriever originated in 1860 when Sir Dudley Majoribanks of Brighton, England, purchased eight performing dogs from an Eastern European circus troupe. Those dogs were called Russian Trackers and were accomplished trick dogs.

According to that report, these Russian Trackers were used chiefly as guard dogs to protect the great flocks of sheep in Russia's Caucasus Mountains. The strongest and usually the biggest dogs were chosen to combat the flocks' predators. These dogs often measured 30 inches at the shoulder and weighed more than 100 pounds, and those with the heaviest and thickest coats were most valuable because of the cold Russian weather. Those dogs, so the story goes, were the ancestors of the first Golden Retrievers.

However, most current authorities say that sometime before 1865, the (now extinct) Tweed Water Spaniel was used as foundation stock for the Golden Retriever. This spaniel was crossed with Irish Setters and other hunting dogs, small Newfoundland dogs and probably Bloodhounds to produce today's Golden Retriever. All this cross-breeding was done in an effort to produce a superior gundog with just the right combination of characteristics: trainability, toughness, courage, good swimmer, protective coat, ability to find downed birds in thick cover, gentleness and willingness to relate to people and take direction. Today's Golden Retriever is big and tough enough to satisfy outdoors people and gentle and trainable enough for families with children.

Why does my Golden love to swim?

You tend to like what you do best. So do dogs. Most dogs are proficient swimmers, and for many years Golden Retrievers have been selectively bred for swimming ability and a great love of water. That means you will have a hard time keeping your Golden out of any nearby lake, pond, stream or swimming pool.

Leg strength, body musculature, coordination and balance are among the qualities that make the Golden a superb swimmer. Other retriever qualities, such as good scenting ability, soft mouth (holding a bird in his mouth without crushing it), obedience, temperament and coat quality, accompany his swimming ability.

How big do Goldens get?

Males stand 23 to 24 inches at the withers (the tallest point of the shoulder), and females are a couple of inches shorter. In other words, a male Golden's shoulder is knee-high to a six-foot man. When he's standing with all four feet on the floor, his muzzle can usually reach a steak lying on the kitchen table. Coffee table treats disappear quickly when a Golden strolls across the room. An adult Golden standing on his hind legs is as tall as a petite adult human, and a rambunctious Golden can easily knock over a child or an older person. Some Goldens grow taller and some shorter and, like humans, some lean toward heavyweights and others are slim. Balance and muscularity are more important than size in this sporting dog.

What does physical balance mean?

An adult male Golden should appear powerful. He should be slightly longer than he is tall, measured from the foremost point of his chest to the rear of his buttocks. A Golden should be strong, full-bodied, standing on sturdy legs, with a muscular chest and rump. His head should be broad and somewhat massive, and his neck should be muscular. His physique should appear smooth and balanced, never clumsy-looking. His movement should be easy and graceful, and his legs should be well muscled as befits an athletic dog who can earn his biscuits by swimming with a duck or goose in his mouth.

A female Golden's features are balanced as well, with considerable strength and coordination, but her muscle mass should be more refined and her weight a few pounds less than the male's. When you look at a Golden, you should be able to discern the difference between male and female at a glance, even though they're performing the same work.

How active are Goldens?

Goldens are not super-energy individuals, like small terriers, but a healthy Golden will need plenty of vigorous exercise each and every day. A Golden pup will be moderately active, but usually your puppy is as active as you *allow* him to be. A pup's activity may feed off his family's activity, and if he's playing with energetic children, he'll be a living dynamo until he exhausts himself or is confined. A typical young adult is a reasonably active individual as well, and can keep up with almost any human activity.

A healthy adult Golden of any age who's living with a family that has several children probably won't need any more regular vigorous exercise than he gets playing with the kids—*if* the children play with him just about every day. A Golden one to fours years old should be exercised vigorously at least once a day for at least half an hour, and also should go on at least two leisurely walks every day. A Golden five and older will need at least three walks every day, plus a half hour of vigorous exercise a few times a week.

When your Golden is asleep, he's busily planning his next game in his dreams. If you're looking for a sedate lapdog, a very low-energy pet, the Golden isn't the dog for you. But you can redirect his constant frolicking.

Teach him new activities. He'll enjoy it just as much as pointless playing, and you'll both get a feeling of accomplishment.

Why is a Golden puppy so active?

Because he's a happy camper! A Golden puppy's merry attitude is contagious, and his playfulness and curiosity are timeless. A healthy Golden's desire to frolic is quieted only by old age. The innate desire to play begins as soon as a puppy is coordinated enough to tackle a sibling, and it never disappears. The Golden has a happy switch. He can act serious and reserved one minute and be roughhousing the next. He'll curl up beside a sleeping child and be quiet and content there until the child begins to stir, then will spring to life, ready for any adventure. A big, active puppy can get rough, though, so very young children should not be left alone with a Golden pup.

Are Goldens good watchdogs?

If you want a guard dog or protection dog, look in another direction, because the Golden isn't the dog for you. A Golden has a big voice and may announce a stranger at the door or gate, but when it's a neighbor or friend calling, she'll greet them affectionately. Guarding property is foreign to a Golden's character. However, a watchdog's job really is just to warn her family of an approaching stranger, and this can be learned by a trainable Golden.

Do Goldens shed a lot?

Without regular, frequent combing and brushing, a Golden is a hair merchant. His hair isn't short and stiff like a Dalmatian's or a Pug's (that kind of hair sticks on everything), but it collects in nooks and corners of the house in little golden dust bunnies. This breed probably isn't for you if the first question you ask is "Do they shed?"

What does a Golden need from me?

A Golden Retriever is a friendly, people-oriented, loving and lovable dog who bonds tightly with his owner or handler. He'll trust you if you are consistent and patient with him, and will be a trustworthy companion if you give him the training he deserves.

Your Golden Retriever is a pack-oriented animal, like his wolf ancestors. When he comes to stay at your house, he has traded his canine pack for a human pack, and he wants to be included in practically all of his family's functions—even if it means just watching. A Golden wants to share and be included, and will eventually exhibit behavior problems, and even health problems, if he's penned or tied up or otherwise regularly excluded from family activities. Some Goldens are quite happy just going for an afternoon ride in the country once a week, going on a picnic or driving to a lake or park. If you spend two hours a day with your Golden in between such functions, he'll be ecstatic.

He's a living paradox. He'll sit for hours for petting and grooming, but *you* must manage his coat or he'll shed copious quantities of hair every day. His favorite pastimes include fetching, playing ball, chasing and romping with children, and he is rarely discontented except when *you* ignore him. He will often find a toy and bring it to a family member, sit with it in his mouth, waiting patiently, begging to play, but *you* must direct his activities.

He's not picky about what he eats, but you can't keep a Golden happy with food unless it's followed by a long walk, a swim in the lake, a game of Frisbee, or some quiet petting time shared with a member of his family. He wants a yard, but the yard furnishes only the opportunity to play. Play must involve you and other family members. A Golden needs his humans to toss a ball for him; a hide and seek game requires human participation.

Goldens demand training. Since they have active minds, they'll become bored and think of mischief. They need challenges and to be taught a new concept nearly every day. It needn't be a complex problem-solving venture, and might be a simple child's game of hide the toy under a rug.

Although a Golden isn't terribly conceited, to look his best he'll need regular grooming all his life. You should brush his coat twice a week, and each session should last about 20 to 30 minutes, or until his coat is straight, untangled and shiny.

Grooming is an activity that Goldens anticipate with enthusiasm, once they learn its advantages. They're no different from other dogs who enjoy the personal handling and touching that accompanies regular brushing and combing. Few doggy chores require as much conversation as grooming, because Goldens like to be talked to and they like the one-on-one dialogue that accompanies grooming.

Why are Goldens so people-oriented?

Prehistoric dogs hunted in clans or packs, usually made up of relatives. Dogs have been selectively bred from those who considered themselves part of *human* society, and the Golden has risen to the upper crust of dogs who are extremely people-oriented. He assumes his role in a human pack and lives contentedly there. One breed rescue organization referred to Goldens as "Velcro dogs" because they do best when they're close to their owners.

Do Goldens think and reason like we do?

That depends on how *we* think. Dogs have varying abilities to store experience, think, reason and solve problems. Goldens have sharpened those abilities over many years of selective breeding. An 1895 training book written by Mr. B. Waters noted that most dog owners of his day believed dogs' actions were only related to instinct. Waters flatly stated that premise is woefully *wrong*. A dog's actions are related to his *knowledge*, which depends on heredity, training and experience.

Dogs have fantastic memories, and they use that to great advantage in learning. Dogs watch their mothers and copy her actions. Thus, if a Golden's mom is a gentle, loving, well-socialized and peaceful pooch, he will have that pattern to follow.

Reasoning and planning result from inherent intelligence, learned cleverness and past successes. When a Golden hunting dog discovers that *wounded* quarry dive and swim away quickly, he'll retrieve them first, before picking up those that fall to the lake like a stone and are obviously dead. Reasoning also is exemplified by a Golden's rushing to pull a floundering infant from a lake. A Golden guide dog will refuse to take his blind handler onto a trail that leads under overhanging tree branches, even though the dog's height is well below the danger. Those situations can't be taught, and are the result of reasoning and planning.

Why are Goldens so popular?

Goldens are people pleasers. They are number two on the American Kennel Club's breed list because smart people want smart dogs. Popularity depends upon personality, size and maintenance requirements, and the slow-maturing Golden Retriever is a smart dog with an easygoing personality. He's typically intelligent, athletic, clever, self-confident and trainable.

There is a perception that Goldens don't shed much, but in fact, they shed as much as any dog and require their share of maintenance. Good nutrition and regular grooming will help minimize shedding.

There is also a perception that the Golden Retriever is the end-all, perfect companion who doesn't require anything except food, water, and housing. Wrong, wrong, wrong! It's natural for you to think of the obvious attributes a Golden Retriever offers, but at the same time, you must consider his less desirable imperfections.

The Golden Retriever breed has many genetic problems (see Chapter 4), so buying one requires very thoughtful screening. A Golden is quite intelligent, but many people consider him slower than some dogs of other breeds. Usually he's extremely trainable, but he still requires patience and consistency, exactly like any other dog.

Sometimes Goldens' popularity clouds the mind of a shopper. Maybe several of your friends have smart, lovable, beautiful and wonderfully trained Goldens, but a neighborhood trend is a lousy reason to acquire a living being. If you find that status is your true motive, buy a classic Mercedes or a yacht instead of a loving Golden Retriever.

Why are some owners dissatisfied with their Goldens?

They refuse to accept a Golden for who she is. They think they're getting a perfect, trained, non-shedding, super dog—which the Golden is not! Often, dissatisfied owners want nothing in their life that's as unpredictable and time-consuming as a companion pet, no matter how loving she is.

What is the Golden's share of the United States dog population?

Exact numbers are impossible to calculate, but according to American Animal Hospital Association surveys, there are about 52.9 million dogs in the United States. These dogs live in about 31 million households, so each dog-owning household averages about 1.69 dogs. Those surveys report that approximately half the U.S. dog population is purebred.

The American Kennel Club (AKC) recognizes 150 different pure breeds, although worldwide about 400 breeds are recognized. The Golden Retriever ranks number two in numbers of AKC registrations (after the

Labrador Retriever), with 63,497 Goldens registered in 2001, out of a total of 1,081,335 AKC-registered dogs. This means that about 6 percent of *all* registered dogs in the United States are Goldens.

Annual Golden registrations are down from 1997, when the number reached over 70,000. Many Golden fanciers believe this decrease is healthy, because even after a breed loses some of its popularity, conscientious breeders continue to select the best dogs for the gene pool. Therefore, the decrease might mean that fewer but better breeders are producing fewer but better Golden Retriever puppies.

How long do Goldens live?

Never long enough to suit their owners. Barring accidental injuries and serious illnesses, a typical Golden will live 10 to 13 years. His life span depends upon genetics, nutrition, exercise and preventive health care.

If you choose your puppy carefully, feed him appropriately, and take good care of his health, he should live at least a dozen years and maybe longer. As a puppy grows, his needs change and you must adjust his diet and exercise accordingly. As he continues to age, his requirements change dramatically. You must adjust a senior Golden's care to accommodate his physical changes, and failure to do so may cause your pet's life to end prematurely. Mistakes made during puppyhood may return to haunt you and your Golden in later years and shorten your pet's life.

How does human age compare with dog age?

The oldest dog in the world was an Australian Cattle Dog who lived 29 years and five months (don't expect your Golden to approach that record!). Large dogs have a shorter life expectancy than small ones.

The first year of a midsize dog's life is approximately equivalent to 21 human years, and each subsequent year of a dog's life is roughly equivalent to four human years. By this calculation, a six-year-old dog compares to a 41-year-old human, and a 10-year-old dog compares to a 57-year-old human. Since the Golden is a fairly big dog and has a correspondingly shorter life expectancy than smaller dogs, he may even be a bit older at age 10. Let's just say that a 12-year-old Golden Retriever is well into his Social Security years.

How long do Goldens stay puppies?

Some breeders and owners say Goldens never grow up. It's true that they mature more slowly than many other breeds, and this slow maturation rate is more prevalent in males than females. Usually puppy silliness begins to slowly diminish from about three to six months until about two years old in females. An individual male may retain his puppy attitude longer, until well after physical maturity.

A Golden should never be considered a ready-made companion, and he will require significant training before all his kinks are worked out and replaced with the habits that typify his breed. Your Golden pup wants to be a good companion, but until you teach him otherwise, he doesn't know that he should chew or take into his mouth only *his toys*, and not your hands and everything else he encounters. Likewise, you must teach him not to jump up on his playmates. He doesn't mean to tear your hose or muddy your slacks, but you must teach him that these activities aren't acceptable.

According to one Golden rescue organization, one of the main reasons for giving up a Golden is that a family with young children doesn't always have time to devote to obedience training. When that happens, by the time the Golden is full grown, he's nothing more than an oversized knucklehead. Buyers almost always underestimate the amount of personal time a Golden requires. When a family with small children applies to this group for a Golden, the request is often discouraged because children lose interest quickly. If you're thinking of a Golden for your kids, DON'T! He always will be *your* companion and *your* responsibility.

Why is there so much difference between a Golden show dog and a Golden pet?

You can enter any AKC-registered Golden Retriever in AKC-sanctioned events. In that way, there is actually no difference between a Golden show dog and a Golden pet. However, from the very finest litters of Goldens raised by expert breeders, only a precious few will win ribbons and titles in shows. Those are the cream of the crop, the very best Goldens. They score high in show competition because they conform closely to the breed standard, which describes a perfect Golden Retriever.

Is a Golden's coat color an indication of his quality as a show dog?

No. The coat of a show dog is part of the physical appearance that makes him a show dog, but it's not the only part. Show judges frown upon white or extremely pale colors, and many top dogs are darker shades of gold. But the show dog's general musculature, leg strength, head and neck size and shape, joint angulation, stride, carriage and character all contribute to his winning ways.

Is there a difference between hunting Goldens and pet Goldens?

All Golden Retrievers have many ancestors who were hunting dogs. These dogs weren't much different from the pet dogs of today, except that their masters lived at a time and in a place where pheasants or ducks abounded. Those Goldens truly paid for their keep by putting birds in the hunter's bag, thereby putting meat on the table and money in the bank.

Today, field Goldens are selected based on their physical ability to do the hard work of retrieving shot birds, their trainability, and their heart and desire. A field Golden is likely to be a more active dog who requires a higher level of physical and mental stimulation.

What are the top 10 reasons people want a Golden Retriever for a pet?

1. They are outdoor people who want to share their activities with an easygoing, affectionate pet.
2. They want a happy and responsive dog who looks for fun instead of dog fights.
3. They want a loving pet who loves petting and cuddling.
4. They want an obedient dog who will obey house rules about children, elders and dogs.
5. They want an intelligent dog who understands and enjoys games of all kinds.

6. They want a trustworthy and trusting pet who thrives on human interaction.

7. They want a clever dog who demonstrates problem-solving skills.

8. They want a dog who will join children's and adults' activities with playful exuberance.

9. They want a funny dog, one with a sense of humor who acts silly and clowns around.

10. They want a trainable dog who can be taught tricks and games.

What are the top 10 reasons people give up their Golden Retriever after they've acquired one?

1. "He's too demanding. We didn't know that a Golden required so much of our time. (No, we didn't discuss this matter with the dog's breeder.)"

2. "We wanted a smaller dog, but he was such a cute little puppy in the pet shop window. (No, we didn't ask how big he would be.)"

3. "We thought he would be just fine tied in the backyard. We bought him a doghouse, and he has food and water available, but he just sits and whines. When we turn him loose for a few minutes, he jumps on everyone and is totally out of control."

4. "We can't keep him home. He climbs over the fence every day just as soon as we're gone. When we come home at night there he is, playing with the neighbor kids."

5. "He barks continuously and our neighbors called the nuisance control officers. He didn't bark when he was a puppy and living in the house with us, but since we've confined him to his run we can't control his barking."

6. "He jumped up on the baby, knocked her over and scratched her face. We can't risk any more of that. (No, we didn't teach him not to jump up on children because we thought that would come naturally as he grew up. No, my husband really doesn't have time to train him.)"

7. "We can't afford him. He eats tons and veterinary bills are nearly bankrupting us. We didn't know that Goldens had so many hereditary problems to cope with."

8. "We moved to a small apartment with no yard. We can't play with him all the time. We've considered walking him frequently, but that takes all of our free time."

9. "He sheds too much, especially on the furniture. The carpet is matted with hair and we can't vacuum the rugs because his hair clogs up the sweeper. We tried grooming him, but that's a never-ending task!"

10. "I'm too busy to train him. When I start, he acts thickheaded and just wants to lick my hand. I've lost my patience and he just sits there looking wistfully at me."

What kinds of people will best be able to develop a Golden into a good pet?

Active people who like to spend a lot of time doing things out of doors. Smart, patient people with a well-developed sense of humor who are devoted to their companion. Those who appreciate an intelligent, trainable dog and will spend the necessary money to acquire a fine, healthy representative of the Golden Retriever breed. They will take the time to train her appropriately, care for her properly, both mentally and physically, and mold her personality into that of a desirable pet. They will offer the dog love and attention, and will acquire the knowledge and take the time to ensure that their Golden receives suitable nurturing, training, grooming and discipline. They'll appreciate their companion's admirable qualities and will treat her with respect, even when correcting a problem.

What kinds of people will probably have difficulty managing a Golden Retriever as a pet?

Couch potato people who don't enjoy physical activity. Impatient and uninformed people who seek shortcuts to everything. Fussy folks who have little time for their pets. People who want ready-made solutions to all problems and can't or won't take time to work on solutions. Demanding people who expect their dog to obey every command immediately, if not sooner. People who don't understand a Golden's sensitivity, intelligence and abilities. It's disheartening to learn that nearly 20 percent of all dog owners are dissatisfied with their pets and consider them more trouble than they're worth.

Each Golden is a thinking, reasoning individual. They have similar temperaments and share some physical characteristics, but each has her own special character. A Golden isn't a pre-programmed robot who has been assigned the chore of pleasing your every whim. Therefore, each Golden must be managed as a distinctive personality in a special, unique way. This takes time, patience and lots of love and caring.

Why shouldn't I want a Golden?

A Golden Retriever is a time sponge who will soak up all the hours you can give. He's a smart, happy companion, but not a worry-free creature who's perfect in every way. He's a loving canine pet who will return every speck of affection you give, but to do so, he'll need training and extensive socialization. He sheds, too, so he'll need lots of grooming to minimize the amount of hair he deposits on rugs and furniture.

2

How Does a Golden Retriever Behave?

How do adult Golden Retrievers behave as pets? • What is typical Golden puppy behavior? • What is *acceptable* Golden behavior? • What is a Golden's attitude toward being a house dog and family pet? • How are Goldens with children? • How are Goldens with older people? • How are Goldens with people who aren't members of the family? • How are Goldens with other family pets? • Are Goldens aggressive toward other dogs? • Are Goldens aggressive with people? • Are there special behavior problems particular to Goldens? • What is the general temperament of Goldens? • Can my Golden live outdoors? • Can I safely leave my Golden home alone while I'm at work?

How do adult Golden Retrievers behave as pets?

They will behave exactly as they did in the whelping nest, *unless* you teach them what's acceptable and what's not. An adult Golden does not come equipped with the attributes that make a great Golden. She becomes a delightful pet only when a well-informed owner has taught her good manners. An untrained adult Golden will snack from your kitchen counter. She will not remain calm when meeting strangers unless you've taught her to be calm. She won't knock over children if you've trained her to keep all four feet on the floor. She'll be impeccably housebroken only if you've taken the time to teach her where to go. Goldens are very trainable, but you must spend time training them.

What is typical Golden puppy behavior?

A Golden Retriever puppy is playful, loving, cuddly, likes to sleep briefly on your lap and would love to climb into your bed. She sniffs imaginary and real trails, rarely barks, is easily startled by noises but not often frightened. She loves interacting with children because she perceives them as siblings and thinks she can outsmart them. The downside of this is that she nips at her siblings as part of normal play, and you will have to teach her that it is unacceptable to nip at children.

Like all pups, Golden puppies alternate between periods of extreme activity and long naps. They are easily excitable, and can be wild and destructive if they are not properly supervised. Constant monitoring, removing all breakables and consistent, patient training will help you get your puppy under control, but all puppies somehow manage to chew on forbidden items, have housebreaking accidents and knock things over, no matter how much you supervise. Plenty of playtime will help use up some of that puppy energy. Retrieving games are favorites, but Goldens like any activity that includes human participation.

They are a little afraid of being carried, even by adults, and they squirm from the grasp of children. And remember that Goldens are slow to mature, so puppyish behavior may persist even into their second year.

What makes a puppy chew everything in sight?

Golden puppies, who have a strong retrieving instinct, investigate their environment by mouthing it. That includes your toes, the books in your bookcase, your best shoes on the closet shelf and virtually every other object that will fit into their mouth. The best way to avoid having your things chewed is to keep them out of reach and make sure your puppy has appropriate chewing toys.

The best way to avoid having your hand chewed is to immediately substitute a toy for the finger he's targeted. You need say nothing to him; scolding is always a bad idea, but if you feel you *need* to say something, you can tell him *"NO"* in a normal but decisive voice as you remove your finger from his sharp little teeth. While he's a puppy, it's always a good idea to have at least one small toy in a handy pocket.

With proper training, the puppy's mouthing and chewing habits gradually disappear as he creeps into adolescence during the first year. By the time he's a year old, he should be gaining the personality features of an adult. But if you're lucky, he'll still clown around and make you laugh until his muzzle is gray.

What are the behavioral differences of puppies from different backgrounds?

No pup is born with perfect deportment, and from the very first day of his life, a pup's mother teaches him canine pack rules, correcting and sometimes chastising him when he misbehaves. He also receives his dam's love and kindness. This balance sets a standard for pack manners that last a lifetime.

Orphan puppies raised in the absence of all other dogs totally lack pack manners and may be difficult to correct or control. They're not antisocial, but are actually asocial and lack any knowledge of canine social discipline.

If one or both parents are aggressive, irritable, shy and lack all social graces, their puppies probably will follow in their parents' footsteps. They won't easily adjust to their human families to become pleasing and agreeable pets. The acorn doesn't fall far from the tree.

Human socialization is another reason for behavioral differences. A pup will have better social skills if she's raised by a breeder who spends lots of time with his litters. Interaction with people should start as soon as possible, and a conscientious breeder begins handling all puppies shortly after birth. The Golden pup absorbs *human pack* rules of conduct very early and will learn the smell and touch of her handler, begin to trust him, and actually start to display affection for him even before her eyes are open.

To perpetuate this social discipline, specific rules of conduct must be consistently followed in your home. You should combine love and petting with teaching, just as your pup's mother and the professional breeder did. Training should begin as soon as she comes into your home and should include housebreaking, simple commands and crate or pen training. All teaching endeavors should be undertaken calmly, and with patience and respect.

What is *acceptable* Golden behavior?

Breeders and rescue organizations say a Golden Retriever of any age should never display surliness or hostility toward other dogs or humans, and should always be reliable and trustworthy. Timidity or nervousness isn't typical of a Golden's character. Solid gold temperament is the hallmark of the Golden breed. This doesn't mean every Golden meets this standard. It means every Golden *should*. Certainly, there are Goldens who do not.

Beyond that, whether your Golden's behavior is acceptable depends on what role she will play in your life. If she will be mainly a companion, you want her to show good manners, playfulness, friendly greetings and genial charm.

If she's to be a gundog or a field trial retriever, she should still have all the qualities of a companion, but her work dictates that she conduct herself in a slightly different manner. Gundog training begins early, and by weaning time she may be introduced to scented and feathered toys and canvas retrieving dummies. Shortly after she has received her final puppy vaccinations, she may get her first experience smelling gunpowder, encounters with living birds, fetching from water and swimming. Far away gunshots may be heard when she's only a few weeks old, and the guns are brought nearer as she becomes accustomed to their sounds. Her inherited retriever instincts develop very quickly, and the Golden soon begins to act like a gundog.

You'll know when you meet a gundog. She's more aware of your clothes and accouterments. She's still happy to see you even when you are wearing a business suit and carrying a briefcase, and she will shower affection upon you as always when you arrive home from work. However, her gundog greeting is different. When she sees you in boots, wearing hunting gear and carrying a shotgun case, she'll stick to your side like

Velcro because she knows she's going to share your day. The well-trained hunting Golden loves the smell of gunpowder and will sleep on a hard floor beside a shotgun in a hunting cabin. Of course, she'll also be quite at home stretched out on the soft carpet beside your bed when you return from your hunting trip.

What is a Golden's attitude toward being a house dog and family pet?

Gundog characteristics exist in all Golden Retrievers, but these inherited attributes may be dimming with each generation of Goldens. Today's Golden is first and foremost a family companion. She bonds tightly with her human pack and usually is equally attached to everyone in the family. When you choose her with temperament and trainability in mind, she should be the happiest dog in town even if she's not out hunting—and you'll be even happier.

Do Golden house pets miss having ducks to hunt?

Canine communication hasn't progressed to the state where we can answer that question with any certainty. Probably most Goldens would like to try their paws and jaws at hunting and retrieving, but very few of today's house pets would care to live the life of a hunting dog year-round. A Golden loves to retrieve canvas dummies and tennis balls. Hunting and retrieving still are, and always will be, a Golden's instinctive traits, but he doesn't need shotguns and live birds to be happy. Goldens are rapidly becoming comfort-seeking creatures who prefer a nice warm hearth and a walk in the park on a brisk wintry day to a plunge into an icy pond.

How are Goldens with children?

How are *children* with children? Most kids are curious, gentle, loving and playful. With those kinds of children, a Golden will thrive, and both dog and child will benefit because their temperaments are so in tune. If a child is cruel, rough or abusive, the Golden may try to escape, whining, squirming away and hiding. And if she finds herself cornered, she may bare her teeth and threaten. An adult should closely monitor *all* play time between small children and dogs.

It's important to remember that just as not all children are good with dogs, not all dogs are good with children—not even all Goldens. The average dog views the average child as another dog, and that means nipping and roughhousing as he would with a littermate. That's why if you have very young children, it may not be wise to get a Golden—or any dog—until the children are a little older.

What should I do to make sure there's no danger to the child or the dog when they're together?

You can expect a puppy to do exactly what she feels like doing, unless you teach her differently. This same presumption applies to a child. A puppy will invite children to participate in games with her toys, but you must *teach* her not to jump up, mouth or chew on the kids' clothing. Similarly, you must *teach* children to pet and play with a pup using appropriate toys, but not to squeeze, drop, hit or poke the pup, and *teach* them not to encourage jumping up. Remember, a full-grown Golden is a big dog who can easily knock over a child. If you and your children discourage jumping games when your Golden is a puppy, you will avoid this problem when she is an adult.

What special training do my children need?

It's the responsibility of all the adults in your household to teach the dog and the children what they need to know about interacting with one another, and to monitor their association closely. You should reinforce both the pup's and kids' lessons until you're satisfied that good conduct will reign when you're not watching. Under those conditions, you should expect no danger to child or dog.

If you have an infant and your Golden is a tiny puppy, there's no reason for any training except the normal instruction in good manners that every pup needs. Your dog will be nearly a year old and have a great deal of routine training behind her by the time the infant is a toddler. Then, when the child has reached the age of squeezing pups and doesn't yet understand your instructions not to, your Golden will be clever enough to escape and hide. When the toddler is agile enough to catch the pup, your Golden will be strong enough to withstand most of his advances. At that point, the Golden isn't likely to be hurt unless the child knocks over something and it lands on the pup.

If the child has reached toddler age or beyond and the new Golden is a tiny pup, the usual puppy training is necessary (as always). But additionally, you must give the child some specific instruction. Herein lies an inherent problem: Children are given soft, furry, squeezable stuffed toys to play with. They look real, and some stuffed dogs actually bark and walk. Playpens are lined with those delightful toys. Toddlers poke little fingers into their lifelike puppy's eyes, toss it against the wall, use it like a hammer and try to pull off its legs and ears. Needless to say, you must guard against this kind of learned behavior at all costs and protect your new Golden puppy. Your child must understand that a puppy is not a toy.

Start by making sure he understands that his actions are capable of scaring or hurting a puppy. Remind your toddler that although he is little for a human, to a puppy he seems like a giant.

Instruction takes only a few moments each day, and a little of your time will reap a lot of rewards. Teach each child in the family how to properly approach and pet a puppy, leaving the pup on the floor. Show your toddler how to sit on the floor and hold the puppy on his lap. Insist that he never lift and carry your Golden puppy. Take the time to teach older children about the advantages and benefits of pet ownership and care. Watch them carefully, and correct their mistakes immediately but tenderly. Give them some responsibility for the dog's care, but *never* leave it up to your children to make sure the dog is properly cared for. That is *your* job.

Teach all children to respect the pup as a living creature. Tell them about the pup's need for naps and quiet time. Teach them to appreciate the pup's response to careful handling and petting. Allow mutual respect to develop between all ages of children and your Golden, and everyone will appreciate your kindness and consideration. Failure to spend the time and insist on those house rules will surely return to haunt you in the future.

How are Goldens with older people?

Full-grown, well-trained Goldens can be wonderfully patient with a senior who may have lost some physical coordination and move heavily or unsteadily. Goldens are popular visitors at nursing homes, where a senior citizen who loves dogs and wants to associate with a Golden will appreciate her good humor. Your Golden actress will try her best to convince the older person that she hasn't received this much attention for eons, and the senior will love every minute of her performance.

Remember that a Golden can knock over a frail adult as easily as she can a child, so make sure your Golden is properly trained — especially about not jumping — before you introduce her to older friends or family members.

If a senior is thinking about getting a Golden as a pet, it's important to remember that these are active dogs. Of course, there are active seniors, as well, so each individual match must be considered. A senior who can take their Golden for several long walks a day, or play fetch for half an hour in addition to three or four moderate walks a day, will do fine with a Golden. But often a young Golden, and especially a puppy, is too much for a senior to handle. Consider a senior dog for a senior person — many wonderful older dogs have a tough time getting adopted simply because of their age — but remember that even a Golden who has slowed down somewhat still needs moderate exercise every day.

How are Goldens with people who aren't members of the family?

A stranger will be accepted if he displays the recognized body language of a friend, speaks in low tones, offers a hand for her to sniff and doesn't insist on immediate interaction with the dog. This kind of introduction is just common sense when meeting any dog. A typical Golden, when greeted this way, will wag her tail, drop her ears and turn on the sad-eyed charm. Then it's the stranger's turn to prove he's worthy of your Golden's acceptance.

While Goldens are not overly protective, they will respond to your body language and tone of voice. So if you do not readily accept the stranger, chances are neither will your dog.

How are Goldens with other family pets?

A successful sporting dog has a strong instinct to chase prey, and a Golden is no exception. Goldens are not good pets for people who live around livestock and poultry, and they may also chase small animals such as cats, rabbits and even small dogs.

Are Goldens aggressive toward other dogs?

The Golden Retriever is among the least aggressive breeds known. They are excellent companions and guide dogs because of their trustworthiness and compatibility with other dogs and humans. However, when a female is in season nearby, a male may display aggressive tendencies that are usually directed toward other males. Sometimes a rescued dog from an abusive home is defensively aggressive, but these kinds of dogs should be placed with experienced dog owners and not in a novice home.

Are Goldens aggressive with people?

A well-bred, well-socialized Golden Retriever should not be aggressive. However, aggression in Goldens is a growing problem in the breed that must be acknowledged. Rescue organizations and shelters probably see a greater number of aggressive Goldens because the population of dogs they work with is made up of Goldens who have been given up by their former owners. Lifelong training can *sometimes* manage aggressive tendencies in *some* dogs, but an aggressive dog is not what anyone wants for a pet.

What's the difference between mouthing, chewing and biting?

Mouthing is a puppy behavior in which your Golden takes into his mouth various objects to taste them. It's a learning behavior that has nothing to do with chewing. Chewing is a destructive vice, and includes munching on the coffee table, tearing the spines off your first-edition books and/or shredding your pant legs. Biting is the purposeful sinking of the dog's canine teeth into an animal's body to hurt or kill it. A dog bites out of aggression, fear, self-defense or because she's been trained to do so.

What does *soft mouth* mean?

It's a necessary trait for gundogs, and refers to the ability to carry a game bird so gently and carefully that its flesh isn't damaged. It pays off in companion dogs as well, because Goldens with an inherited soft mouth are easily trained to stop mouthing hands, chewing furniture and tugging at pants legs.

Are there special behavior problems particular to Goldens?

The desire to retrieve is very strong in the breed, and this can lead to a dog who will bring you everything in the house, from books to underwear to bathroom towels. Training will help you solve this problem, but it's wise to keep things out of reach of a new Golden puppy.

Because Goldens have such a strong desire to interact with their families, they may also tend to grab an owner by the arm to lead them on an adventure. You *must* nip this behavior in the bud, because what seems like innocent fun to your dog could become quite painful for you.

What is the general temperament of Goldens?

A Golden Retriever generally has an admirable temperament — she trusts you, and you can trust her to act in a dependable way. Your Golden's temperament includes a great sense of humor, which means she is fun to be around. She is very dependent upon her owners. You must encourage and reinforce these positive aspects of her temperament all her life.

Timid or aggressive Goldens are rare, as this is not typical temperament for the breed. But this doesn't mean there are no such dogs. When you find them, avoid them and their puppies.

What's the difference between behavior and temperament?

Behavior relates to a dog's conduct in human culture and is principally a learned set of traits that well-informed dog owners can teach their dogs. A Golden's behavior in the human family depends on her purpose for being there and what's expected of her. If she's primarily a companion, she must behave like one of the family. If she's strictly a hunting dog, the conduct rules are a little different. Behavioral problems are the most common reason for giving up a purebred dog.

Temperament is mostly inherited, but it's partly learned. It refers to a dog's attitude, her inherent disposition or the way she reacts to everyday circumstances. A Golden's temperament is the way she treats you, other people, animals or events. It's her *mode of emotional response* to various situations. Your Golden's temperament might be described as gentle and trusting, suspicious and defensive, or somewhere in between.

Why is temperament so important?

Because your Golden's temperament will affect your ability to trust or distrust her actions. Predictability is what you're after. You want to be sure of her response in all situations, so you must know her temperament. If she has an inherently sour or unpredictable temperament, she'll likely be unfriendly, unpopular and not trustworthy in human society.

How can I determine my prospective Golden puppy's temperament?

Meet and handle her parents. The temperaments of a pup's parents are the best indicators of their puppies' dispositions. Watch her dam and sire (if you can; often a pup's father is owned by a different breeder and will not be on the premises) to see if they accept you without undue suspicion. Then watch the litter. If a puppy comes wriggling to you, wags her tail and licks your hand, that's an excellent indication. If she invites handling and responds to your quiet whistle or voice, that tells you she's likely to be a friendly sort.

What is the best way to evaluate temperament in a puppy?

It's difficult to analyze temperament differences between puppies of the same litter because they're usually playing, seeking laps to sit on, fingers to chew and faces to lick. In other words, they are all focused on you. Stand back and view the litter through the crack in a door. Observe their interactions with one another and note any who seem shy. A timid pup should never be your first choice—or, for that matter, your second or third choice.

A shy pup tends to grow up into a shy dog—afraid of strangers, skittish and difficult to handle. Shyness can also lead to fear-induced aggression.

Watch for the intimidator of the litter. A bully pup is a poor choice because this domineering trait may be impossible to soften. Look for a happy, curious pup, one who plays with her siblings but isn't determined to win every battle. Choose the pup who's a bit mischievous, but tends more toward being laid back and less toward overactive.

Professional temperament evaluation hasn't yet become standardized, but knowledgeable breeders, shelter personnel and rescue organizations often conduct personality or temperament tests. If you want, you can also hire a professional trainer who can help you evaluate a dog's temperament—for a fee, of course. Remember that a positive test result doesn't guarantee that a particular Golden puppy is perfect for you. It cannot predict the behavior of a dog in all situations, and cannot factor in the training and experiences the pup will have as he grows. If you decide to hire a pro or personally evaluate the pup's temperament, the result must be used only as a tool, not as the definitive selection criterion.

Not all temperament tests are the same, but many include holding each puppy on her back for a short time to see if she trusts human hands and submits willingly. Each pup is petted and handled excessively to determine her level of socialization, then is placed on the floor as the tester walks away. If the pup follows him, that's a good sign. If she comes when called, that's another excellent sign. These kinds of tests should be done by the breeder.

A reputable Golden breeder will also evaluate *your* temperament, background, age of children, home size and type of work, including your free time. Ask the breeder if he thinks your family fits a Golden's needs, and if so, which of the pups in the litter he thinks best matches your needs.

Is any dog's temperament totally predictable?

When you consider all the possible interactions and conditions a dog may come in contact with, the answer must be no. But what you really want is a Golden with maximum predictability under *normal* circumstances. I knew a big Golden male who was a totally predictable companion except when he was managing a yard full of children. He allowed only parents to intervene, and if a stranger approached too closely, the big dog would challenge with bared teeth and force the stranger to back away. This wasn't a response to training and isn't instinctive for an easygoing Golden, but probably someone encouraged the behavior the first time it surfaced, so it persisted.

A dog of any breed may behave unpredictably under extreme conditions. How a Golden will react to physical pain or perceived danger to himself or his family is always a question, and depends on the degree of pain that's being inflicted and the dog's protective instincts.

Another unpredictable behavior is running in a pack. One dog is a pet, but more than one constitutes a pack. When a pet Golden is allowed freedom to run and roam, and falls in with another dog or two, the result is a pack of dogs. In a pack, each dog loses his individual behavioral character and all members act together to create mischief ranging from intimidating innocent people to chasing and even killing animals.

Rescued dogs usually are predictable because, as adults, you can see their temperament most clearly. However, in some instances events of the past may interfere with predictability. For example, if a man in coveralls abused the dog in her former environment, she may treat all men in coveralls with suspicion, or even aggression.

Can a faulty temperament be changed?

Purebred dog breeders consider abnormal temperament to be one of the top 12 most important issues in any breed. Temperament is essentially an inherited characteristic, and it cannot be altered. However, some behavior problems that result from poor temperament can be managed. Shyness is a good example of this. Lifetime training to manage a temperament problem requires plenty of time, the patience of a saint and the assistance of a professional. A pro can also help you determine what type of problem you can manage and live with, and what type you cannot.

Sometimes what is perceived as a faulty temperament is really a training or behavior issue (or unrealistic expectations about what a dog is capable of), and these are much easier to deal with. Discuss any problem with your Golden's breeder and your veterinarian, and listen to their advice. If the temperament problem is real and serious, such as aggression, you should consult a professional trainer.

How common is bad behavior in Goldens?

Unacceptable behavior is the most common reason for any purebred dog to land in a shelter. Golden Retriever rescue organizations are reluctant to re-home an aggressive or untrustworthy Golden because of the associated liability. Between 10 and 17 million dogs of every description enter shelters in the United States annually, and between 4 and 9 million of those dogs are humanely killed, either because a home could not be found for them or because they are unsuitable as pets.

About half of all purebred dog owners have discussed a behavioral problem with their veterinarian. Behavioral problems vary in importance. They may just be simple nuisances, such as house soiling, barking, jumping up, chewing or minor property damage. More serious behavioral problems include aggression, separation anxiety and defensive behavior.

The quicker the problem is discovered, the quicker it can be resolved. If you're facing a behavioral problem, don't delay in getting help to resolve it. A long-standing bad habit usually will take a correspondingly long time to alter because a dog must unlearn the bad behavior and, at the same time, learn an acceptable substitute.

Can my Golden live outdoors?

Can *you* live outdoors? Probably, but do you really want to? Your Golden is part of your family. If you have a companion who trusts you and wants to share your home with you, why exclude her? If you can't tolerate hair on your carpet and footprints on your tile, perhaps you should consider a goldfish. Very few Golden Retriever owners live in homes so perfectly organized that they can't happily tolerate a little doggy influence.

In addition, Goldens are susceptible to skin problems, and total outdoor living may aggravate these problems. Some fear lightning and thunderstorms and become anxious at the gathering of clouds. Others are stolen from yards while you're gone or during the night, and some leave on their own by digging under or climbing over fences.

Why aren't Goldens good outdoor dogs?

Physically speaking, they are. They have thick, double coats for protection, and most have enough body fat to survive all but the most severe winter weather. With a good doghouse to provide shelter in the cold weather and shade when it's warm, your Golden is physically equipped to be an outdoor dog.

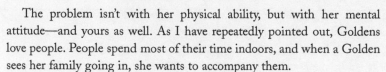

The problem isn't with her physical ability, but with her mental attitude—and yours as well. As I have repeatedly pointed out, Goldens love people. People spend most of their time indoors, and when a Golden sees her family going in, she wants to accompany them.

If you don't allow her to come inside with you, your Golden will reluctantly accept whatever you offer. But when you look out the window, you will see her standing there, ears down, wearing a sad expression and begging to come inside and be with you. Dogs are pack animals, and they cannot live alone. Goldens, who are particularly people-oriented, suffer greatly from isolation from their families. The boredom and loneliness can literally drive them to extremes.

Isolation also initiates a downward spiral of behavior. In other words, if you leave your dog outside because she doesn't behave well in the house, she will never learn to behave well in the house, and her behavior will also become wilder and wilder outdoors because she will be so excited to see you and interact with you when you come out to visit her.

A Golden needs training, attention, affection and a family to live with. And all those things are inside.

Can I safely leave my Golden home alone while I'm at work?

Yes, but with conditions. A crate or pen inside the house is essential for a small pup, and a friend or neighbor must take her outside several times a day. A puppy of eight weeks shouldn't stay in a crate for more than three or four hours without being taken outside. After three months, a crated pup will usually stay clean and happy for four hours without being taken out. A young adult of 9 to 18 months will tolerate being left crated for six to eight hours, but she won't like it. Always try to make arrangements to have her taken out at least once every six hours.

A working family's home for an adult Golden will ideally include a doggy door to the backyard and a rugged perimeter fence to securely contain her. It should also prevent all intruders from jumping over, chewing through or digging under—which rules out invisible electronic fencing.

What are the dangers of leaving a Golden at home?

The dangers are few if you've carefully considered your dog's needs. That means not giving your young dog free run of the house until she has been thoroughly housetrained and has learned what is and is not appropriate to chew. It also means picking up all loose items (shoes, knickknacks, etc.) your dog may be tempted to chew on or could accidentally knock over, and covering or hiding things that cannot be removed (such as power cords). The dog should also have plenty of fresh, clean water and appropriate chew toys.

Separation anxiety, where a dog becomes overly anxious when she's away from her people, should also be mentioned. Dogs with separation anxiety can become so anxious that they destroy the house or even chew on themselves. This terrible syndrome isn't common in Goldens, but sometimes it begins when a dog has bonded too closely with her owner and becomes too dependent on him—and that can surely happen with such a people-oriented breed. Some of the things humans inadvertently do to contribute to this syndrome include:

- Making a big deal out of leaving for work, such as long good-byes and rattling the car keys.
- Leaving home by the same door and at the same time every day.
- Being gone for eight or more hours at a stretch.
- Providing no amusement for your Golden while you're gone.
- Allowing her no outside access during your time away.
- Making a big deal out of returning home, such as immediately petting, feeding, giving treats and having lengthy conversations with her.

In short, separation anxiety usually begins when you make your Golden extremely aware that you are leaving and that when you return she'll get unlimited attention. When these factors creep into your routine, watch out for the evolution of a Golden wrecking machine.

Separation anxiety usually appears gradually. First, she'll begin whining and barking, and neighbors will tell you all about that. Next, you might find the threshold of your front door scratched and chewed. Then she may deposit urine or feces near the door by which you left. Then she may shred newspapers, books or any other items in the room. That minor vandalism progresses to more serious damage to furniture and especially to the curtains on windows by which she can see you as you leave. Extremely anxious dogs may chew on themselves or lick an area obsessively until they develop a bald patch.

What can I do about separation anxiety?

Some corrective procedures include:

- Stagger the times you leave, even if it means going to work very early one day and late the next.

- When you leave, don't tell your dog good-bye. Don't rattle your keys or otherwise call attention to your leaving. And vary your routine: Give her a couple of toys and a treat one day, but not the next. If possible, don't leave by the same door every day.

- Leave early, return in an hour or two, stay for 15 minutes, then leave again. If your work schedule doesn't allow that, try this routine on weekends.

- Stagger your total time away or break your absence into two periods, if possible. If you can't do this, hire a friend or neighbor to stop in to check on her, take her for a quick outing or toss a ball a few times.

- Hire a professional dog walker. Be sure to check his references and instruct him to take your Golden out several times a day.

- Install a doggy door, if possible. Of course, this means having a strong, escape-proof fence.

- Leave her a large, interactive toy full of yummy kibble.

- When you arrive home, first tidy up the room, hang up your coat, take a shower, change your clothes and generally ignore your Golden for at least half an hour, then take her out for a leisurely walk. Don't immediately make a fuss over her, feed her or tell her she's a good dog.

These measures will minimize the importance of your being away and returning, and your intelligent Golden should soon learn to accept the situation. The hardest part is ignoring her when you arrive, but you can do it, and the results will more than justify the effort.

3

How Will My Golden Retriever Grow and Develop?

What's unique about a Golden Retriever's physical development? • What's unique about a Golden Retriever's mental development? • How much canine socialization does a Golden puppy need? • How much human socialization does a Golden puppy need? • What can I expect from a developing young adult Golden? • Are adult Goldens always predictable? • At what age is a Golden considered a senior citizen?

What's unique about a Golden Retriever's physical development?

Golden Retrievers develop slowly compared to small dogs. The skeleton is usually completely formed shortly after one year of age, but mental and muscular development and coordination isn't reached until they are nearly two years of age, and sometimes much later.

A Golden female reaches sexual maturity later in life than a little dog, and her first ovulation usually occurs shortly before one year of age. Usually a male is capable of breeding when he is between 8 and 12 months old. (Don't count on those figures for contraception; individual dogs vary greatly in the age they reach sexual maturity.)

What physical development will I see from weaning to three months?

At weaning age (about six weeks old), a Golden is a funny, fat, round puppy who is playing clumsily all the time. Puppies of the same litter develop at varying rates. In some breeds it's hard to tell one pup from another, but at birth, each Golden puppy has his own appearance and rarely looks exactly like his siblings. One's coat may be lighter in color or a little thicker, for example.

How does a puppy develop before weaning?

A puppy is born with his eyes and ears closed. His eyelids begin to separate and open at about 10 days of age, and the ear canals open a day or two later. A Golden puppy can perceive sound at birth because his auditory function is present even though his ear canals are sealed. He can distinguish his dam's sound, scent and touch on the first day of life. He's like a heat-seeking missile, and he immediately begins crawling around, moving toward his mother's warmth and that of his siblings. He finds his dam's nipples by scent and touch immediately after birth. By two weeks of age, his eyes are fully open, his hearing is more acute, and his olfactory system is quite developed. He begins walking more or less upright by three weeks of age, unless he is extremely fat. Walking may be clumsy for another week if he's a rotund retriever.

At three months of age, a pup loses some of his puppy fat and begins to gain coordination. He'll climb stairs, but won't be able to go down again without help. His baby fat continues to fall away between four and five months, and he'll begin to chase shadows and follow birds that are flying overhead. A five- to six-month-old Golden is a typical gangly teenager with largish feet and is often slimmer than you expect him to be.

The phase that extends from six months to a year finds your Golden's puppy fat diminishing, as it is replaced with firmer musculature. During this period his body continues to smooth out, his feet appear to fit his body, and his baby hair gradually changes to a thicker, straighter, flatter coat. You will see a definite improvement in his coordination and ability to run, pivot, jump and land squarely on his feet. He begins to take his fetching lessons more seriously, can swim for hours, and nearly always remembers to return his retrieving dummy to your feet and release it when he arrives.

When will my Golden puppy be ready to housebreak?

As soon as he enters your house, but don't rush the program. Instinct tells a wolf that her den shouldn't smell like wolf dung, so the dam trains her pups to deposit their bodily waste as far as possible from the nest. A Golden is born with similar instincts that call him away from his sleeping and eating places for elimination. You should build upon that hereditary virtue by taking him outdoors frequently to a spot where he has previously defecated and urinated. Have patience, be consistent and he'll do the rest. (See Chapter 7 for a complete discussion of housebreaking.)

How fast will he grow?

A Golden ordinarily grows in spurts. He shoots up suddenly, then coasts for a week or so. Just about the time you think he's destined to be a small dog, he grows like crazy. He usually reaches his maximum height between 12 and 18 months of age and attains his maximum weight and strength by 24 months. Development and growth are related to genetics and individual nutrition, and no standard data apply.

How can I make sure he'll be as big as possible?

A Golden Retriever is a larger medium-size dog and try as you may, he'll never be a giant. Optimum size for each individual is primarily inherited and you can't change it by feeding your dog more or less. Don't try to force your Golden's growth!

If you feed him an adequate amount of the appropriate premium food, he'll eventually be as big as his genes will allow. If you overfeed or overexercise your Golden during the growing phase of his life, he may suffer consequences that will be disastrous to his health and your veterinary budget.

How can I help my puppy develop into a strong, muscular adult?

Monitor his physical development and activities and make sure he stops when he shows any evidence of tiring or slowing down. Until he reaches full maturity, you shouldn't allow him to exercise strenuously for long periods of time. Walks on a leash are fine, but running beside a jogger or a biker is not advised. Racing around in your backyard is OK, but endless retrieving is dangerous. His willingness and attempt to please you mean he'll to try to keep up with everything you ask him to do, and his wonderful appetite will allow him to gorge endlessly. But an overexercised or overweight puppy risks bone, ligament and tendon deformities because his weight and heavy activity overwhelm his immature, soft cartilage.

Regular exercise is critical for any dog to ensure normal physical and physiological function. Exercise is also quite important for mental development, bonding, general health and digestion. Your dog's reasoning experience and problem-solving ability are enhanced with exercise, and exercise will also help minimize aging changes. (See Chapter 8 for more information on a Golden's exercise requirements.)

What's unique about a Golden Retriever's mental development?

Goldens have an enormous need to be with people. A Golden who develops into a fantastic companion will absorb your time like a sponge. He'll reach that stage of perfect pet only if you devote loads of time to him and use that time productively. Failure to give *yourself* to him unselfishly while he's a puppy will make it impossible for him to achieve his true potential and become a great Golden Retriever partner.

Mental skills develop a little more slowly in the male Golden, and often a female is a more serious thinker and is quicker to respond to problem-solving tests. Some four-year-old males are unsophisticated and act quite puppyish and without dignity, but a female usually has settled down by two years of age.

What mental development will I see from birth to three months?

A puppy's mental capacity or learning ability builds from birth onward. His first education is quite rudimentary and principally involves interpretations of touch, sound and smell. For this phase of development, his teachers include his dam, his siblings and perhaps his breeder. Bonding with humans can begin in a newborn if he's regularly handled during that phase.

At two weeks, shortly after his eyes open, he begins to use visual acuity to build upon the first phase of learning, but until about three weeks, his mental discernment is pretty basic. He'll recognize his dam and siblings and perhaps his breeder from afar, and will show excitement when they approach. At about three weeks, he'll begin to recognize strangers on sight and may display fear as well. As he progresses from three to about five weeks, he learns some canine pack rules. By six weeks, he will begin to set his internal alarm clock for solid feeding times and will anticipate those events with relish.

Also, by six weeks he'll begin to find solutions for some of his minor problems, such as how to find the up ramp into the whelping box and, depending on how much territory he is allowed to range, will be able to find his way back to the nest immediately. At seven or eight weeks, he should have the measure of the pack's pecking order and know whom he can dominate, and just how many liberties he can take with his mother before he receives her reprimand.

By 8 to 10 weeks, he's able to understand and obey simple commands, learn his name and recognize voice modulations and some body language. He'll follow his ball when you toss it, but he will probably just mouth it for a minute when he picks it up. He will remember short training sessions with few lapses, and some puppies are totally housebroken by 12 weeks of age or before. This entire process of mental development is gradual and differs from pup to pup, but your Golden's cleverness may reach high levels by the time he's three months old.

How can I find the Golden puppy of my dreams at this tender age?

Choosing just the right puppy for you at this developmental stage is difficult. A big male might attract your attention because of his beautiful dark color, wavy coat and mischievous nature. A petite female might be quicker, a bit lighter in color and a little less active, but she could be just the puppy you're seeking.

Ask your breeder what she has named each puppy. Probably she's given them temporary names related to each pup's attitude toward his siblings, and that might tell you more about the individual personalities than any test you could perform. She may call a particular male Caesar because he's ambitious. A petite female might be named Cinderella because she's developing into a special lady. Another is called Hercules for his balance, size and strength, and perhaps another is Plato because he sits and puzzles at each new turn of events. Sometimes knowing these temporary names will tell you a lot about a pup's personality and help you decide which puppy is best for you.

Don't choose a shy, timid, aggressive or overly rough puppy because those pups often lack the social skills they need to be fantastic companions. Laid-back puppies often develop into more trainable adults than the clever, speedier ones. In the final analysis, though, your best puppy probably is the one who chooses you.

Trust the reputable breeder to ask you what you expect from your Golden when he's fully mature. She then will list the probabilities of development for each puppy in the litter. You'll be amazed at the differences she points out, and what these differences might mean to you.

What mental development will I see from three to 12 months?

Between three and four months, your Golden will begin zooming from room to room and rug surfing on tile floors. He'll love to chase balls and toys, but will probably chew them when he catches them. At the magic age of four to five months, a Golden adolescent will love to fetch, and training should begin to perfect the game. Between five and six months your Golden will watch you toss his ball, fetch it, bring it to you and, with a little training, will drop it at your feet.

Mental development from six months to a year depends on the Golden's personality and how much attention you pay to his training. It isn't a matter of heredity alone. Mentality also depends on his experience and exposure to both positive and negative situations.

As the months go by, his learning ability gradually begins to firm up, just like his muscularity. Generally, a six-month-old Golden is expected to comprehend many training exercises, he has often started to hunt, and he can solve many somewhat complex problems on his own. He learns to escape from confinement, to jump up on footstools, then chairs, then to the end table to reach the candy dish. You are honing his retrieving skills if you practice them often enough, and he may be retrieving inanimate objects and sometimes ducks from the water long before his first birthday. He has sufficient mental capacity to learn obedience commands and to master the techniques of running agility courses and flyball contests, although a youngster less than a year of age seldom excels in either.

By a year of age, he should have learned the basic skills and acceptable manners he needs to survive, and perhaps thrive, in his human society. He should have mastered the human pecking order, know when to persist and when to relax, and will infrequently overstep his bounds. One problem you might encounter is that a Golden is clever enough to try new solutions to old problems. He might remember exactly what to do to perform a certain task, but the next time you present it, he may decide to try a different approach. Owners often misinterpret such action as stupidity, when in fact it is simply the Golden's attempt to circumvent boredom by inventing a new procedure.

What kinds of lessons will aid his mental development?

Your tutoring should begin the day he arrives and continue until old age. (See Chapter 7 for details about training a Golden Retriever.) He must first learn his name. Then he'll tackle some household manners and learn a few simple commands, such as come, sit and a few others. A simple command is a single request for a specific behavior. When you are teaching each command, you should expect your Golden to quickly comply. For example, "come" means to hurry to your side, "sit" means put his bottom on the ground, and so on. Each of these commands is complete by itself, but when you're living with a Golden, it's best to teach two or three at a time, perhaps as part of the same training session, perhaps in alternate sessions. For instance, first you teach his name, which is meant to get his attention and his focus on you. Then you tell him "Spot, come," which is actually two commands. When he arrives, you tell him "sit," which can sometimes follow the first two commands in sequence and sometimes be practiced on its own. Soon he has learned a whole vocabulary of commands, and also understands that they can be shaped into a sequence of behaviors.

A Golden's training should be specific and directed to make the best use of his attitude, but you can discourage a great attitude at any time if you give him an impossible (for him) task that sets him up to fail. In other words, try to tailor your training to your dog's mental progress; challenge his mind, but don't ask the impossible.

How does a puppy's physical growth correlate with his learning abilities?

Each phase of a puppy's physical and mental development is matched with changes in his competence. Your Golden pup wants to please you, so you must use that instinctive trait to your best advantage.

At first, his attention flits from this to that and his imagination is stirred by every little movement or sound. As his mental capacity develops, you'll notice that he focuses on you more closely while you're walking and talking to him. He still notes each squirrel that moves, but he's more composed and thinks a second before he rushes headlong to the end of his leash. That's his signal for you to begin to offer him new challenges, such as obedience exercises, among others.

His problem-solving abilities are rudimentary when he's only a few weeks or months old, but as he gains coordination, his competence and understanding also increase. By three to four months of age, he'll welcome challenges that include more complex games and instruction, and by five or six months of age, he'll approach a formidable task with a can-do attitude. These ages aren't the same for all dogs, and your Golden's problem-solving ability at any age depends on the number and variety of challenges to which you expose him. Within reason, the more you ask him to do, the more quickly and more cleverly he'll respond.

How much canine socialization does a Golden puppy need?

In the wild, dogs continually meet others of their kind. In today's protected society, you must furnish the opportunity for your Golden puppy to meet other dogs of every age, size and disposition. Although sometimes harsh and unpleasant, his canine socialization experiences are critical to his development into a great companion. He'll gain knowledge of how dogs live by socializing with other canines while still a pup, and will be able to better interpret the personality of each dog that he meets in the future.

Just as there are some things you can't learn from a book, you can't hope to teach your dog to tolerate and respect other dogs by yourself. His inter-canine communication skills need to be developed, and this requires your Golden pup to meet other dogs. *You* can't be the teacher because that role belongs to another dog.

Puppy kindergarten classes are definitely a step in the right direction. You can expand upon kindergarten lessons by taking walks with friends and their dogs. It's your Golden's job to learn, but you must always be on hand and ready to protect him. His instincts usually will save him from confrontations, and he'll learn appropriate postures and body language from older dogs. He'll also learn his limitations and how to submit graciously to more powerful dogs.

A Golden who isn't given the opportunity to explore canine interaction is apt to become timid, shy or aggressively defensive. A reclusive, introverted Golden isn't accepted into canine group classes such as obedience and conformation shows. He doesn't last long in competitive sports, is difficult to handle in many other circumstances, and usually makes a lousy gundog in the bargain.

In some respects, American dogs miss an advantage that European dogs enjoy. In many of those countries, dog owners walk their dogs off-leash, and loose dogs meet one another each time they go for a daily outing. Many human gatherings include canine friends, parks are filled with people and dogs, and yet dog fights are extremely rare. Those dogs are canine-socialized from puppyhood throughout their lives, and consequently they accept unfamiliar dogs without fuss.

How much human socialization does a Golden puppy need?

Human socialization is the single most important duty of responsible Golden breeders and owners. When you acquire your Golden puppy, he's a raw resource, a pound of ore that has a rich potential but hasn't been developed or refined. He needs cultivation, not reinventing, modification, not rebuilding. He's inherently perceptive of human needs and has the right genetic makeup to become a sympathetic and cooperative companion. If you let him develop naturally, mold and nurture him carefully, you'll happily share the next dozen or more years with him. However, unless he's given your guidance and leadership during his formative years, he'll never develop into your ideal pet.

You must allow your Golden to spend as much time as possible with you and your family. Accept him into social events as if he were a growing child. You should handle him gently, with care and above all, with kindness, and without physical reprimand.

If you feel like strangling him because of some *faux paws* he has committed and you really want to impress him with your strength and dominance, tell him "*NO!*" in a gruff voice, then turn and walk away. Leaving him alone is perhaps the worst punishment you can offer a Golden. He's a sensitive little guy, and will be dumbfounded by being ignored. He'll follow in your footsteps, seeking forgiveness and will remember your actions for a long time.

This rule should be followed in all cases where he is disobedient or careless, but don't hold a grudge. Never give him the impression that he won't regain your confidence. After ignoring him for a few minutes, change the subject. Ask him to sit and shake hands, then forget your differences and play catch or toss his favorite tennis ball.

What can I expect from a developing young adult Golden?

Just about anything goes. Goldens are inventive and clever, and they'll amaze you daily, but not always in ways you expect. You can get a brilliant response to training exercises one day, and the next day his hard drive will crash and he'll act like a cucumber on a leash. You'll note that his sense of smell is outstanding, and when he remembers to use it, the results are delightful. If you're alert, you can expect your young Golden to teach you a great deal about himself—more than you ever expected to learn.

Are adult Goldens always predictable?

A Golden adult is about as unpredictable as his owners are. This is a part of his character that's inborn and never lost. Eventually you'll figure him out, but not completely. Just when you believe you know exactly what he's thinking and what he's going to do next, he changes the rules. This applies to working Golden gundogs as well as companions and competition dogs, and it is one of the joys of a human-Golden partnership. His unpredictability always keeps you thinking and ready to meet his challenges.

Your Golden isn't apt to do anything irrational or really stupid at any age of development, but he may fool you by taking the wrong turn while on an agility course. He may crawl under a jump instead of going over it. He might decide to wander off and sniff an interesting spot when you told him to stay. He acts that way just to reassure you that he's an individual with a unique personality, and will do just what he will do. In a way, you can predict that he'll always be unpredictable.

I once hunted with a beautifully trained Golden with a fabulous nose who suddenly began acting strangely. He hesitated, stopped and showed intense interest in a pile of sunflower stalks a dozen yards ahead of us. We couldn't see a bird but trusted the Golden's nose, so we waited, guns ready. His handler finally told him to go, thinking he'd jump the bird. The dog dove into the pile of stalks, snatched up a field mouse by its tail and returned to his embarrassed handler, who received the wriggling rodent into his hand as if it were a pheasant. It was even more embarrassing because the mouse was the only game we caught that day!

At what age is a Golden considered a senior citizen?

When he begins to slow down from age alone. A typical Golden's muzzle begins to turn gray at about 7 to 10 years, although it may be earlier. After reaching his golden years, he'll still enjoy doing just about everything he did as a young dog, except that it will take longer. When your Golden's age tells him to take it easy, he'll be content to take a patriarchal role in your family, but he'll really be upset if you exclude him from your activities.

What can I expect from a senior Golden?

The Golden oldie looks at you a little less clearly, but he'll still rise with a creak to greet you when your eyes open in the morning. He'll wag his tail, but won't bounce around as you get out of bed. He'll stiffly follow you from place to place, a tennis ball visible in his graying muzzle, and he'll fetch it once or twice if you don't toss it too far. When your footsteps interrupt his afternoon nap he won't leap up, but his tail will still thump the floor. His walks in the woods will be a little slower, but he will love a brief swim in the lake when the water's warm. He won't pursue sassy chipmunks or chattering squirrels, but will pause for a moment to watch them and wonder if he still could.

Are senior Goldens' physical changes associated with mental decline?

Most definitely. An olden Golden develops arthritis, vision and hearing problems, all of which may affect his actions and reactions. When your Golden begins to show signs of physical deterioration, step back and re-evaluate his diet, his activity, his resting places, his access to your home and every other phase of his physical life.

Watch for frequent soft, runny stools, or hard, claylike or chalky stools. Those signs mean his digestion is somehow impaired. He should be examined by a veterinarian, who may want to adjust his diet, add supplements or formulate a new diet. If he walks laboriously, hates to get up for his walk or limps, he needs to be checked for joint disease, bone tumors or soft growths that infringe upon joints. If he lies down at the foot of stairs or takes all day to climb up the four steps into your house, he probably has one or more joint diseases, and you can help him with a ramp to make climbing more gradual and easier. If his temperament seems to be souring with age, senile dementia may be the cause. Ask your veterinarian to evaluate his physical and mental health. You can add years of enjoyment to his senior years with some simple modifications.

4

How Healthy Are Golden Retrievers?

 How healthy are Goldens in general? • What do genetics have to do with a Golden's health? • What are some hereditary conditions that affect Golden Retrievers? • How common are allergies in Goldens? • How much will it cost per year to keep my Golden healthy? • How do I find a good veterinarian? • What vaccinations does my Golden need? • Do I have to spay or neuter my Golden? • What if I want my female Golden to have puppies or my male to be a father? • Do all dogs have worms? • Do I need to worry about fleas and ticks? • Why does my Golden scratch her ears all the time? • Why is my old Golden losing her hair on each hip and on her elbows? • What is heatstroke?

How healthy are Goldens in general?

General health is tied to genetic health, and you cannot speak of one without the other. A Golden who is born genetically sound and receives appropriate preventive health care should have few physical problems. However, her soundness of mind is as important as her physical and hereditary soundness. Balance all three of these factors and you'll have a healthy Golden Retriever.

What do genetics have to do with a Golden's health?

A great deal! Genetic planning begins with the decision to breed a specific dam to a specific sire. It also includes your precautions when you select your puppy. If you choose the best pup from an inferior Golden litter, what do you have? A mediocre pup with a shaky background! However, if you select a pup whose parents are at least two years old, have no hereditary faults, are in perfect physical health and are proven winners in some Golden endeavor, you have an excellent chance to obtain a phenomenal companion.

How important are hereditary diseases, and can they be treated?

Genetically transmitted diseases can be mere nuisances or they can be disastrous. Some hereditary diseases can cause blindness or permanent lameness, and others may be fatal. Some can be successfully treated and *most* can be eliminated by careful breeding practices that only use dogs who have been certified free from the hereditary diseases.

What are some hereditary conditions that affect Golden Retrievers?

The complete list is long, so only the most important or most frequently diagnosed problems are presented here, alphabetically.

- Cataracts are inherited among families in a significant number of Goldens, and in many cases they are not apparent to owners. Removing the cloudy lens is sometimes helpful.

- Elbow dysplasia is a hereditary condition that occurs when the elbow joint is improperly formed, and it eventually becomes apparent when the Golden becomes lame. Surgical repair is possible and sometimes totally effective.

- Entropion is an inherited eyelid condition in which the eyelids roll inward. It is usually diagnosed when a Golden's eyes frequently tear excessively. Surgical repair of the condition usually will give excellent results.

- Hemophilia A, or AHF deficiency, is inherited and causes prolonged bleeding and hemorrhagic episodes.

- Hip dysplasia is a very common hereditary disease that often occurs when careless breeding is practiced. The hip joint is improperly formed and causes arthritis and difficulty walking. Surgical repair or joint replacement is possible in some cases.

- Hypothyroidism is an inherited autoimmune disease of Goldens that occurs when the hormones of the thyroid gland diminish. It can be treated with daily medication.

- Moist dermatitis is a surface bacterial infection that may result from allergic skin disease that's considered hereditary in Goldens. Ongoing treatment is necessary for good results.

- Osteosarcoma is bone cancer, the predisposition for which is hereditary in most large breeds. Goldens are at risk for this cancer, whose first sign is a lameness, accompanied by swelling and tenderness of the bones. It usually occurs at the ends of the long bones of the skeleton. Treatment is difficult. Other cancers, especially lymphosarcoma (cancer of the lymph nodes), have also been occurring with increased frequency in the breed. Certain families and bloodlines seem to have a higher incidence.

- Progressive retinal atrophy (PRA) is an inherited eye disease of Goldens and many other breeds in which central vision is lost between three and five years of age. It's a hereditary disease, and there is no known treatment that can restore vision.

- Subvalvular aortic stenosis (SAS) is a hereditary circulatory defect, occurring in the aorta immediately outside the heart, and is being diagnosed more and more frequently in purebred Goldens. Successful treatment is rare.

- Von Willebrand's disease is a hereditary blood disease similar to hemophilia A, and it causes prolonged bleeding. Therapy is tedious, but some relief is possible.

Why are there so many?

Golden Retrievers have been quite popular for a number of years. Popularity means a great number of owners will buy *any* dog who looks like a Golden Retriever. That leads to careless breeders, out to make a quick profit, who have invaded the Golden ranks. They breed every Golden, regardless of its faults, and this fact alone perpetuates hereditary diseases.

Well-meaning but negligent amateur breeders can also contribute to the problem when they find an average pair of dogs, breed them and sell the pups through newspaper ads. (See Chapter 9 for more information on breeding.)

How is modern genetic research helping Goldens? It's absolutely mindboggling! Much has been learned about hereditary diseases, cancer and autoimmune diseases in the past few years. Additionally, surgical techniques are more sophisticated, and canine surgeons are better trained and use better equipment today than in the past.

People's attitudes about their pets have changed, as well. A hereditary disease that was fatal 20 years ago may now be handled with relative ease if the owner is able to pay the bill.

More importantly, genetic research has shown that it's possible to eliminate or minimize many hereditary diseases by careful selective breeding. Conscientious breeders are producing fewer Goldens with hip dysplasia, PRA, allergic and autoimmune diseases and other debilitating conditions.

What can I do if my Golden has a hereditary disease?

If you think your Golden has a genetically transmitted disease, ask a veterinarian to confirm the diagnosis. This might involve sending diagnostic test results to a national certifying organization or a specialist. If corrective therapy is possible, go for it. If your dog is in constant pain and hopelessly beyond relief, other options should be investigated. Under no circumstances should a dog with a hereditary disease be used for breeding.

Should I tell the breeder if my Golden has a hereditary disease?

Absolutely! It's very important to make him aware of the proven problem in your puppy. If he's reputable, he won't allow a repeat breeding of that dam and sire, and your call will initiate further investigation into the genetic composition of both dogs. If the disease jeopardizes your companion's life or function, the breeder should share the cost of a new Golden puppy.

How common are allergies in Goldens?

Golden Retrievers have a very high risk for inhaled, topical and food allergies. These conditions may cause itching, vomiting or diarrhea, and are often quite difficult to diagnose and even harder to treat.

My Golden vomits a lot. Is that caused by an allergy?

It may be, and if it is, diagnosis must be made without delay. Other conditions may cause repeated vomiting, so don't draw any conclusions until you have seen the veterinarian. You'll need to give him an extensive history about when vomiting began, specific food that you have been giving the dog, treats and snacks your dog gets, her activities, changes in drinking water and any other recent changes in her life.

What is a lick granuloma?

This unsightly lesion often results from stress. Skin allergies, minor wounds, insect bites or other stresses cause your Golden to lick her feet, hocks (the joint on the lower rear legs that points backward—it corresponds to the human ankle) or other easily accessible spots. Her persistent licking causes the skin to erode, and it's replaced by thick, hairless scar tissue that never heals. A lick granuloma is a great challenge to treat and is a common problem in Goldens.

What should I do to maintain good physical health in my Golden?

If you're seeking total happiness with your Golden, buy the *genetically* best pup you can afford, invest in sound *preventive health* care, provide first class *nutrition* and wrap the entire program with *your time*. You'll also need to supply annual veterinary checkups, regular exercise, parasite control, good grooming and a sound mental and physical training program. Do a personal examination once a month and record all potential problems. If you communicate with your dog, she'll tell you what she needs.

How much will it cost per year to keep my Golden healthy?

Golden Retriever breeders estimate the cost for annual healthcare to range from $300 to $700 per year. You should consider health insurance, because veterinary fees vary greatly from region to region and usually depend on what services they include. Factors that influence the annual cost of preventive medicine include how often a dog needs vaccinations, whether he needs parasite control, and whether you live in a city or rural area. Higher fees aren't always indicators of better service or better medicine.

Why are veterinary medicine costs so high?

- Newer medical products always cost more because pharmaceutical companies maintain high fees to recover their research and development costs.

- The cost of attending veterinary college is astronomical. Veterinarians must also carry malpractice insurance, and that fact adds significantly to their fees. Look around and find compatible personalities and reasonable fees. It pays to shop around, even for professional services.

- Specialized veterinary care is quickly taking the place of general practitioners' care, and specialized education costs much more than general practice education—as do the specialized tests and treatments offered.

- Emergency treatment always costs more than preventive care, because emergency clinics are open and staffed day and night and charge for that convenience. Many emergencies are preventable, and prevention is a good way to control costs—and protect your dog.

- It is usually impossible to predict and budget accurately for accidents, diseases and complications from infections. Regardless of how careful you are, occasionally your Golden will get into trouble and need professional help, which may be expensive.
- Nutrition costs rise from year to year. New premium foods certainly cost more than supermarket brands. However, the higher cost is more than compensated for by the superior nutrition—which can save on veterinary bills down the road.

Why do veterinary costs vary so much?

- Your dog's genetic heredity greatly influences what it will cost to keep her healthy. Choose your pup carefully so you'll have a healthy dog from the start.
- Cities usually have higher costs of living than rural areas, so city veterinarians generally must charge more to cover the costs of staffing and running a clinic.
- If you buy canine insurance, the cost varies depending on what insurance company you use and what type of insurance you buy, and it's often unavailable in rural areas. Shop around for health insurance for your Golden.
- Preventive medicine by means of routine in-home examinations and mail-order parasite control products can reduce the cost of keeping your dog healthy. Some breeders even vaccinate their dogs at home. But the availability of those products varies according to state laws, and you must have significant knowledge and experience to effectively handle these health issues yourself.
- Your dog's age is a factor. Puppies and senior dogs are more expensive to maintain than dogs in their prime.

What happens if I don't adequately protect my Golden?

If you have a companion animal, you must maintain her health, and that has a price tag. It may be paid up front or after you discover some complex but treatable condition. If you can't afford a purebred Golden because of what it costs to keep her, please don't get *any* dog—because it costs the same to keep a Golden healthy as it does to maintain the health of any dog.

How do I find a good veterinarian?

Doctors of veterinary medicine are a mixed lot, the same as doctors of human medicine. All veterinarians receive a similar education, but they approach their life's work in many different ways. Choose one who talks to you directly, is straight with you, is willing to answer your questions and will treat your Golden like a dog, not like a human. Avoid veterinarians who speak to their clients through managers and technicians.

Shop around for a knowledgeable veterinarian who is compassionate, kind and understanding. The best way to find a veterinarian is through a personal recommendation. Ask your Golden's breeder, a friend, fellow worker or relative about veterinarians in your area. If you're new to town, look in the Yellow Pages for a few animal clinics or hospitals near your home, and choose at least two or three to contact. Call for an appointment to visit a facility and meet the veterinarian and the staff. If they tell you this isn't possible, hang up and call another clinic.

What vaccinations does my Golden need?

Puppies will need a series of vaccinations. They get immunity to many diseases from their mother's first milk, called colostrum, but this maternal immunity slowly tapers off as the pups get older. While pups still have their mother's antibodies, vaccines are not effective. Since it's not possible to know the exact status of maternal immunity at any given moment, a series of vaccinations will ensure that your pup is safe no matter what the maternal immunity situation.

Do all veterinarians vaccinate against the same diseases?

Not necessarily. What vaccinations the law requires, whether you are in a rural or urban area and the incidence of the particular disease in your area all affect what diseases your dog is likely to be exposed to. The known effectiveness and safety of the individual vaccine and your dog's age and health also affect what vaccines she should have.

To minimize vaccine reactions and reduce unnecessary vaccinations, some veterinarians recommend only core vaccinations. Non-core vaccinations include those that counter diseases rarely diagnosed in your region, and others for which there has been a significant number of negative reactions to the vaccine or inconclusive evidence about the effectiveness of the vaccine.

What does *core vaccination* mean?

Core vaccinations are used against diseases that are fatal, extremely difficult to treat and zoonotic (transmissible to humans). What constitutes a core disease varies according to where you live, where you plan to travel and what you do with your Golden. Generally speaking, though, most core vaccination programs include the following:

- Rabies is a fatal zoonotic disease that's transmitted by saliva from infected mammals. Bats, skunks, foxes, coyotes and other wild animals are the most common reservoirs of infection.

- Canine distemper is an often-fatal viral disease and one that takes many forms. It's found in dogs and a few wild animal species, has no known cure and ultimately causes convulsive disorders. Among dogs, it is mainly found in stray and feral populations.

- Infectious canine hepatitis is a usually fatal viral disease caused by canine adenovirus type 2. It primarily affects the liver. It's also primarily a disease of young dogs.

- Canine parvovirus is a deadly viral gastrointestinal disease that primarily affects puppies. It can cause gastrointestinal distress, dehydration and heart problems. The disease can be fatal, and is highly contagious and easily transmitted via the feces of infected animals.

Use of core disease vaccinations means fewer vaccinations are given, and there is growing evidence to suggest this is a good idea. But it also means that each owner must be aware of the vaccinations his Golden has received, especially when traveling. If you're traveling to another state with your dog, ask your veterinarian if your dog will need additional vaccinations.

What are the non-core vaccines?

Your veterinarian will help you decide if your dog needs any of the non-core vaccines. They include:

- Canine parainfluenza is a virus that contributes to kennel cough, which is a complex of upper respiratory diseases. It is easily transmitted among groups of dogs living in close quarters.

- Leptospirosis is a zoonotic disease caused by a spirochete organism, which is similar to a bacterium. It primarily affects the kidney, and if diagnosed early, therapy may be successful. It can be spread by contaminated drinking water and its reservoir of infection is sometimes aquatic rodents.

- Kennel cough is a syndrome that may be caused by parainfluenza (or other viruses) and/or *Bordetella* bacteria. It's rarely fatal, but affected dogs cough for several weeks and complications can be very serious.

- Lyme disease is a zoonotic disease that's transmitted by blood-sucking parasites such as deer ticks. It can cause pain in joints, severe lameness and some rather obscure signs. The available vaccines have been linked to adverse reactions.

Are annual booster shots necessary?

Certainly, your dog needs regular booster shots. But what "regular" actually means is the subject of much debate. Currently, many veterinary schools are recommending revaccination for the core vaccines every three years. Some are also recommending a staggered revaccination schedule, which means the dog does not get all the shots in the same year. Talk to your veterinarian about your dog's vaccination schedule.

Do I have to spay or neuter my Golden?

You should definitely consider it, because there are health and behavioral advantages. In general, altered dogs behave better and are more focused on training and tend to live longer.

If you spay your female dog before her first heat cycle, it dramatically reduces her risk of developing uterine infections, ovarian cancer and breast cancer. A spayed female will never suffer from the common and dangerous uterine infection of older females known as pyometra.

Heat cycles bring hormonal changes that can lead to personality changes in your female Golden, and they are definitely a mess and a bother to deal with. Even a placid Golden has some personality changes that interfere with training while she's in heat. But spayed bitches have a more uniform and predictable temperament. You can take them anywhere, anytime, and that's a plus in anyone's book.

Males rarely have prostate problems after castration is performed. They are less likely to roam, mark territory (including your furniture), fight, or be aggressive or hyperactive. In fact, 80 percent of dogs hit by cars are unaltered males, and the majority of dog bites to postal carriers are from unaltered males.

Dogs and bitches do not get fat from being spayed or neutered. Just like us, Goldens get fat if they eat too much and exercise too little. And spaying at any age after weaning doesn't affect personality, trainability, disposition, growth or size.

Your spayed or neutered Golden has no innate desire to breed. Interaction with the opposite sex doesn't affect dogs' emotions, and breeding is strictly a biological function to ensure the perpetuation of the species. Remove the breeding organs and you remove the hormones that create the desire to breed.

There are advantages for you, as well. In many cities and counties, licensing fees are lower for altered dogs. And many responsible breeders require their pet puppies to be neutered because they want the gene pool of breeding Goldens to be as healthy as it can possibly be.

What if I want my female Golden to have puppies or my male to be a father?

You should definitely breed your female Golden if she is genetically superior, has won championship points in dog shows and if you have sufficient time, space and knowledge to raise a litter. If your male meets and exceeds the breed standard, has proven his quality in conformation show wins or is a superior gundog, he may be an excellent sire. If those factors accurately describe your situation and you've surveyed the puppy market and found an abundance of good homes for your puppies, go for it.

If not, forget it! As I've already mentioned, careful genetic screening in selecting breeding animals is the only way to ensure a healthy future for the Golden Retriever. Breeders are responsible for every dog they produce, for the entire life of the dog, and that includes taking a dog back if the buyer cannot keep him. When all the breeding, health care, nutrition, equipment and puppy destruction costs are added up, breeders report that they seldom come out ahead financially on any litter they breed.

In addition, one female dog and her offspring can produce 67,000 dogs in just six years, and more than eight million surplus dogs and cats are destroyed each year because there are not enough homes for them—with local taxpayers paying the bill.

Are there good reasons to breed a pet Golden?

There are reasons, but not good ones. They include:

- "I want another Golden just like my Buffy." Unfortunately, that's impossible. Buffy can't produce a pup that's identical to her, because the male to whom she is bred introduces half the genes to the litter. Buffy has a certain genetic makeup, and the only way to produce another dog identical to her is through cloning. While that might be possible, unless you are a millionaire the process lies in the future. A better plan is to contact Buffy's breeder and inquire about getting a genetically similar dog.

- "I want my kids to witness the miracle of life." I've heard this so often and it never ceases to make me wonder. Today, there are many videos available to illustrate all the facets of life, including childbirth. These videos are inexpensive and wonderfully educational, and you and your children can review them as many times as needed for complete understanding. Puppies are whelped at all hours of the day and night, and it's unlikely that your children will be awake. Even if they are present, a whelping dam frequently is nervous, and the presence of an audience may cause her to develop uterine inertia and to stop whelping. That can lead to a cesarean section delivery.

- "I want to recoup the cash I paid for my Golden Retriever." This rarely happens, if you do things right. See Chapter 9 for more information on what a responsible Golden breeder must spend on her dogs. Only those breeders who've been in the business for a long time know how to break even, and they certainly aren't getting rich.

- "I love Goldens." OK, I do too. But are you dedicated to truly improving the breed? Do you understand what that entails? If you love Goldens, the overall soundness of the breed should be your first concern.

What happens when a female dog is spayed?

Spay surgery is an ovariohysterectomy, which is surgical removal of both ovaries and the entire uterus. It permanently stops the heat cycle (estrous), which terminates the dog's ability to reproduce. It is a myth that a female dog will benefit from having a heat cycle before she is spayed, or that she needs to have a litter. In fact, female dogs spayed before their first birthday are 99.9 percent less likely to develop reproductive cancers. A bitch doesn't *need* to be bred for any reason, and she suffers no physical or mental stress from being spayed.

What happens when a male dog is neutered?

Neutering surgery is castration, which is surgical removal of both testicles. A male dog doesn't *need* to be bred and derives no satisfaction from breeding. Mating is simply a response to his own hormonal drive, which is stimulated by the pheromones, odors and physical actions of a female dog in heat.

Do all dogs have worms?

Many dogs are infested with intestinal parasites. Among these are roundworms, tapeworms, hookworms, or whipworms, as well as certain protozoan parasites such as giardia and coccidia. Intestinal parasites derive their nutrition from the dog and in doing so they drain her body of energy and constitute a risk to her health. Intestinal parasites are controllable and treatable and most are transmitted to other dogs by means of eggs that pass from the infested host in her feces. Signs of worm infestation may include diarrhea, weight loss, poor coats, and sometimes bloody or mucoid stools.

Can worms be passed to humans?

Some can, and others can't. Roundworms and hookworms can be transmitted to infants or very young children under certain circumstances, and heartworms also may be a threat. However, the worms routinely found in dogs usually are not parasitic in humans, and common sanitation practices should prevent transfer.

What's the best way to prevent worms?

Nearly every year, new and improved medication hits the canine market. Consult with your veterinarian for the best product(s) for the parasites that are common in your area. Some medicines prevent or kill a group of several internal parasites, and these products are becoming safer to use each year. But while some dewormers are effective against more than one type of parasite, no single product is effective against all of them. That's why you need a specific diagnosis before you can choose the safest and most effective dewormer. Your veterinarian can do this by microscopically examining a stool sample from your dog.

What about heartworms?

Mosquitoes that have sucked blood from a heartworm-infested dog spread these dangerous parasites. When the mosquito then injects the heartworm larvae (microfilariae) into another dog, those larvae grow into adult worms and sometimes reach a foot long inside the dog's heart and major blood vessels. Heart disease is caused by this parasite and is sometimes fatal. Heartworm treatment must be handled by an experienced veterinarian, but there are safe and effective preventive heartworm programs for your Golden.

Do I need to worry about fleas and ticks?

Regardless of its environment, any dog can be infested with fleas. A flea bites its host and laps up the blood that oozes from the wound. Flea saliva is irritating to the dog, hence the dog's continuous scratching. To diagnose an infestation, pass a flea comb through the back hair just in front of the tail and check the debris from the comb under a magnifier. Live fleas are easiest to see and appear as quick-moving, hopping insects. The smaller white oval eggs are not so easy to spot, but the black specks of flea feces are quite apparent.

Ticks are more likely to be found outside the city, but don't rule out empty lots and parks. Ticks in different areas of the country can carry different diseases, some of which are extremely dangerous. It's always a good idea to check your dog carefully for ticks after any walk in the woods.

Where do these parasites come from?

Fleas and ticks live in the dog's yard and home, and only reside on the dog when sucking her blood. Ticks attach themselves to her skin, swell with blood, then fall off to lay eggs in the environment.

There are other external parasites lurking in the environment, as well. Lice are bloodsuckers that lay their eggs on your Golden's hairs and spend their adult lives scurrying around on her skin. Mange or microscopic mites are parasites that burrow in the outer layers of skin and are diagnosed by examining a skin scraping. Ringworm (actually a fungus) and mites are spread by contact with infected hosts.

Can I catch these parasites from my dog?

You can catch some, but not others. Canine external parasites usually are host-specific, which means they prefer to live on a certain kind of animal. A tick, for example, has several life stages, each of which may be parasitic on a different mammal. Adult ticks are less host-specific and occasionally live on humans. Some species of ringworm fungi can be transmitted by contact to people or other mammals. And fleas certainly bite people. But mainly, these parasites live on humans as *incidental* parasites, which means they don't attack us as severely as they would attack a dog.

Why are fleas so bad for my dog?

A flea needs a blood meal to live and reproduce, which means a flea bite always punctures the skin. In the process, fleas can spread other kinds of parasites. They can also set off flea bite allergy, a syndrome recognized in all breeds. It's an allergic reaction to the flea's saliva. Flea allergy dermatitis is a common problem in Goldens, who may have an hereditary predisposition to that syndrome. Signs include severe itching with inflamed skin and red bumps. Dogs with this syndrome suffer a great deal, and it's impossible to control without controlling the fleas.

Why are fleas so difficult to control?

The adult flea lays eggs on the dog, which drop into her bedding or your rugs and hatch into larvae. The cycle from egg to adult only takes about three weeks to complete, and an adult can live without a blood meal for more than a year. In other words, fleas are hard to find and hard to kill.

Insecticidal shampoos of various types kill fleas, but they have limited use and can be toxic. Flea collars were once the way to go, but recently they've become almost obsolete. New flea-killing products are much safer than the old flea poisons and collars, and these products have many different ways of killing fleas. Some use tiny protozoa that eat flea eggs and larvae. You spray these flea-destroyers around your backyard to eat up the fleas in their early life forms. When the flea offspring are eliminated, the protozoan flea antagonists also die off.

Several spot-on preparations penetrate into the fat layer beneath the Golden's skin, and when the flea sucks blood, the chemical kills the flea. Oral parasite killers interrupt the flea's life cycle when the flea bites the dog, and still others repel fleas.

Just for the record, you have probably seen advertisements for ultrasonic flea control systems, which are supposed to drive away the parasite using high-frequency sonic waves, but there's little documented evidence that they work. The same is true for natural flea remedies such as garlic and various essential oils.

How can I tell if my Golden has mites?

Hairless patches on your young Golden's face may be caused by microscopic mange mites, especially if the patches are red, scabby or itchy, and if they're larger this week than they were last week. Take your dog to your veterinarian for a skin scraping. When the scraping is examined under a microscope, the veterinarian can make a diagnosis and begin therapy.

If your young Golden's ear tips are swollen, red and losing hair, the sarcoptic mange mite may be the culprit. These parasites love to tunnel around in the skin of a dog's ear tips. The condition can also be diagnosed with a skin scraping. Mites will require concentrated therapy to cure. Consult your veterinarian.

Why does my Golden scratch her ears all the time?

Goldens' longish earflaps tend to shut off the air supply to their long ear canals. An itchy bacterial growth may start within the ear canal if wax deposits also interfere with the natural flow of air. Dirty water from a lake or pond or foreign material that finds its way into her narrow ear canal may promote bacterial infection. Another possibility is an irritation from ear mites, which are contracted from another animal. Have her itchy ears checked by a veterinarian, and never poke a cotton swab into her ear canal.

Why is my old Golden losing her hair on each hip and on her elbows?

If the lesions don't itch and there are no open sores on their surfaces, probably they are calluses. Those form when a senior Golden repeatedly lies down in the same position on hard floors. As long as the lesions are causing her no discomfort, just pad her napping places with thick blankets and she'll thank you for your consideration. If a lesion is painful to the touch, red, soft and mushy, have it examined because there may be an infection within the callus, which will require treatment.

What is heatstroke?

Heatstroke is an emergency in which your dog is unable to sufficiently cool her body. The onset of heatstroke can be rather sudden, and sometimes it takes only a few minutes to reach an emergency situation. It begins with heavy panting and difficulty breathing. Her body temperature may climb to 105 or even 110° F, and in an extremely short time she'll collapse. Her blood pressure falls and her mucous membranes turn icy blue; she becomes confused, staggers and then becomes comatose.

Your Golden is at risk for heatstroke any time the temperature of his immediate environment is above 100° F. If she can get outside and find some shade and fresh water, she's well equipped to handle hot weather. The worst case is when she's locked inside an automobile in the summer, because the glass of the car magnifies the sun's temperature and the inside can easily reach 150°, even when the day is overcast and the outdoor temperature is in the 80s.

A dog such as the Golden, with a heavy body mass compared to small skin surface area, is predisposed to heatstroke. A heavy coat also complicates a big dog's cooling system. Goldens, like most dogs, also have few sweat glands, which limits evaporative cooling. (Your dog cools her body primarily by panting, during which evaporative action cools her tongue and the mucous membranes in her mouth.)

What can I do about it?

You must take immediate steps to cool the dog down. Get her outside into the shade, or into a cool building. Pour cool water over her body and head or, if possible, submerge her body in a tub or tank. Fan her and lift her coat with your fingers so that her skin will directly benefit from the cooling breeze and water. *Don't apply ice or ice water* because that will tend to close skin pores, shrink her skin's surface vessels and make things worse.

As she comes around, give her small quantities of water and repeat as often as she wants. If possible, measure her body temperature with a thermometer and stop the physical cooling process when her body reaches about 103°, because the cooling will continue after you take her from the water. Her target temperature is about 100°.

Preventing heatstroke is simply common sense. Give your Golden plenty of fresh drinking water. Make sure she has shady places to rest. Don't confine her in the sun or in a car. And don't let her do too much strenuous exercise in hot weather.

5

What Should My Golden Retriever Eat?

Why is my Golden's diet important? • What kind of diet does a Golden need to be healthy? • Do all adult Goldens have the same nutritional requirements? • Are puppies' nutritional needs different? • Do seniors need a different diet? • What are all those special diets I see at the vet's office? • Which dog food should I buy? • Aren't all dog foods pretty much alike? • How do I interpret dog food labels? • How often should I feed my Golden? • Are Goldens big eaters? • Can I feed my Golden treats? • Can I feed my Golden table scraps? • Should I give my Golden leftover steak bones?

Why is my Golden's diet important?

Nutrition affects a Golden's total being, including his physical and mental health, temperament, behavior, trainability, personality, immunity and virtually every other quality of a dog. You can speak of nothing biological that isn't greatly influenced by nutrition. "You are what you eat" is an old saying that deserves repeating. Your companion needs the very best nutrition to function at maximum effectiveness. It doesn't matter if you're a breeder, trainer or a conscientious owner, and what your Golden does is immaterial—he still needs the very best nutrition. I'm not talking about quantity of food, but about quality. No dog can do or be his best if he is cheated nutritionally. If your Golden isn't getting the right vitamins and minerals, or if his protein, carbohydrate and fat intake aren't balanced, he's in trouble in every way.

What kind of diet does a Golden need to be healthy?

Diets are many and varied, but few are as complete, balanced and predictable as premium dog foods. *Bioavailability* is the key to all diets. That word refers to the usable quantity and quality of every dietary element, including vitamins and minerals (see page 65 for more information). Together with plenty of fresh drinking water, a premium dog food will provide excellent nutrition.

What are the essential elements of a diet?

- Protein is made up of amino acids, and 10 of those amino acids are essential for normal dogs' lives. Insufficiency of an amino acid can cause a dull coat, immune deficiency, poor growth, weight loss, and, in extreme deficiencies, death. Dog food containing about 18 percent protein is usually advised for adult dogs, and puppy diets should be up to 25 percent protein. Each Golden over nine years old should be examined. If found to have kidney compromise, his diet should contain less protein but with a higher bioavailability level than other adult dogs' diets.

- Fat of either animal or vegetable origin contains all of the essential fatty acids. Although animal fats are more palatable than those derived from plants, vegetable fat is cheaper, so it is more prevalent in dog foods. Fat is a high-calorie essential nutrient and is easily abused. It contains almost twice as many calories as protein and carbohydrates. Canine diets should contain about 5 percent fat. People often feed higher fat diets and fatty acid supplements to their dogs to improve coat quality, but you should only use those under veterinary supervision.

- Carbohydrate is the most economical of the essential elements, and is derived from plant matter. Dogs have a minor need for carbohydrates, but because carbohydrates are an inexpensive source of calories, nearly all dog food manufacturers use it.

- Water is the fourth essential element, and is at least as important as all the others. Without adequate drinking water, a mammal will dehydrate and die long before it starves.

Aren't all dogs carnivores?

It's true that wolves rarely sit down to a meal of fresh fruit, veggies and rice. However, when a wolf kills an antelope and eats the carcass, he consumes all the vegetable matter inside the antelope's stomach. More importantly, through their long association with us, dogs have adapted to a more varied diet, which includes not only protein, but also carbohydrates from plant sources. So dogs aren't true carnivores, the way cats are.

What vitamins and minerals are necessary in my Golden's diet?

The American Association of Feed Control Officials (AAFCO), recommends 11 vitamins that should be included in all canine diets. It's interesting to note that vitamin C isn't included on the list of required vitamins, because dogs manufacture their own supply of this vitamin. Generally, good dog foods that meet AAFCO requirements contain the necessary vitamins.

If you feed supplements, you should be aware that your dog requires a delicate balance: vitamin A is toxic in high doses; the usable levels of vitamin D depend upon the amount of calcium and phosphorus in the Golden's diet; the rate of absorption of vitamin E depends on fatty acid intake. Usually, a multiple vitamin-mineral supplement will do more good than harm, and may be fed to ensure that your Golden's diet isn't deficient due to oxidation or other factors. Before you give your companion a supplement, though, consult a veterinarian.

The AAFCO nutrient requirements list specific amounts of 12 minerals. One important mineral ratio in canine diets involves calcium and phosphorus, which are necessary for nearly every tissue's function, development and repair as well as the dog's overall growth. Diets should contain between 1.2 parts and 1.4 parts calcium to 1 part phosphorus.

Do all adult Goldens have the same nutritional requirements?

No. An adult Golden's nutritional requirements depend on his age, climate conditions and various stresses, including activity, training and strenuous work or play. Nutrition may even influence his personality. A breeding Golden needs a different diet, and a pregnant dam's requirements change yet again.

How should a Golden's diet be altered during stress?

A Golden under stress usually needs more calories and occasionally may require additional specific nutrients, such as calcium, phosphorus, protein or vitamins. A stressed dog is one who has a heavy parasite burden, is undergoing surgery, is recovering from injury or illness, is exposed to severe environmental conditions, pregnant or nursing bitches and hunting or competition Goldens who work for long hours. The nutrition of these dogs should be individually examined. Most will require more calories every day than the average pet Golden needs.

Each type of stress may require a different nutritional approach, but it's rarely necessary or advisable to change diets or add dietary supplements unless your veterinarian advises you to do so. Generally, only the quantity of food will need to be increased. If you're feeding your Golden twice a day and serving a premium-quality dog food, don't just increase the amount you feed her in each of her two meals. Instead, increase her total daily ration by a measured amount and divide the new total into three meals. More frequent smaller meals are more easily and completely digested, and thus do more good than fewer bigger meals.

Because many Goldens have obesity problems, any time you believe your dog is under stress and needs more food, weigh her every two or three days to monitor weight loss or gain. If she continues to lose weight, consult your veterinarian.

Are puppies' nutritional needs different?

Yes, a puppy's nutritional needs are different from an adult's. The protein and caloric quantity of his food should be balanced to meet his rapid growth needs. Because of their rapid growth, pups up to six months old also require twice as many calories each day per pound of body weight than they will need as adults. You should feed a growing Golden pup a premium puppy food for his first year.

In large breeds such as Goldens, overfeeding a pup has been linked to the development of hip dysplasia and other inherited bone diseases. In Goldens, a slower growth rate and carefully monitored exercise is healthier, because it enables the muscles and tendons to develop at the same rate as the bones. Talk to your veterinarian and your puppy's breeder about how much to feed your pup.

Do puppies need to drink milk?

Like adults, a pup requires free access to drinking water, but he doesn't require milk. After weaning, a puppy needs no milk from any source. And even though most pups like milk, many puppies do not tolerate milk or milk products very well and will develop diarrhea.

Then why don't all puppies have diarrhea when they are nursing?

A dog's milk is much different from cow's milk. Bitch's milk contains only about 3.5 percent lactose, while cow's milk contains about 8 to 9 percent, and most dogs can't tolerate that level. Feeding cow's milk to any dog typically results in diarrhea.

How should I feed my Golden puppy?

When you pick up your pup, the breeder should give you a week's supply of the food your dog is accustomed to eating. Don't change the food for at least several days. If you want to feed the pup something different, mix one-fourth new with three-fourths former food for two days, then half and half for the next two days, then three-fourths new and one-fourth former for two days, and on the seventh day feed him only the new food; the conversion is complete.

He'll need three meals a day for at least six months, and thereafter will get by on two meals throughout his adult life.

Always make sure your Golden pup has plenty of fresh drinking water in a clean bowl. When you buy food and water bowls, buy heavy-gauge stainless steel that you can scrub and put in the dishwasher. Make sure the bowls are big enough for an adult Golden to get his mouth into easily. Build or buy a frame for each bowl that holds it right side up. This will foil your ambitious Golden's propensity to carry his bowl from place to place.

Do seniors need a different diet?

This is a question that is still being studied and debated. It is likely that the energy required for a healthy dog to survive with minimal activity tends to decrease with age. So inactive senior dogs may require less energy and may need fewer nutrients than when they were younger. The size and the texture of dry dog food may also be an issue if an older dog has some dental problems.

Because the digestive system of older dogs is more likely to break down, it's not a bad idea to feed an older dog smaller quantities more frequently. And older dogs will certainly benefit from eating higher-quality, more digestible ingredients and fewer calories if they have slowed down. High-quality dietary fat helps to increase the palatability of food, though, which is especially important in older dogs because they may have a diminished sense of smell or taste.

Some foods for senior or overweight dogs also add fiber to further reduce calories. It's important to make sure these diets still have enough protein and other essential nutrients. Remember, too, that not all older dogs are overweight or less active.

So what's a good old-dog diet?

The time-honored old-dog dietary recommendation is to increase the quality of protein while at the same time decreasing the quantity. This advice is always sound if the status of the old dog's kidney function isn't positively known or if evidence indicates that the kidneys are failing. New research tells us that if the old dog's kidney function is proven adequate, the quantity of excellent-quality protein should be maintained or even increased. However, kidney-function tests should be closely monitored when that is accomplished.

The specific amount of protein an older dog needs, as a percent of his diet, depends on several things, including organ function, individual dietary needs and energy requirements.

It is also a kindness to raise your older dog's food and water bowls at least eight inches off the floor to enable him to eat and drink easily, without bending over.

What kinds of health problems would require a special senior diet?

Chronic interstitial nephritis (kidney impairment) is probably among the primary reasons for old dogs' demise, and high quantities of protein tend to overburden an old-timer's kidneys. Therefore, if your dog has been diagnosed with kidney disease, you will need to reduce the quantity of protein in his diet, but increase the quality, in order to decrease the stress on his kidneys. Watch your olden Golden's urine color and quantity. If it's nearly colorless and is produced in great quantities, he may be suffering from kidney problems, and it's time for a trip to the vet.

Diabetes is another problem that plagues older dogs more often than younger ones—especially if they are overweight. Increased thirst and frequent urination, accompanied by rapid weight loss, are the classic signs of diabetes. A diabetic dog will need a special diet, and may also need regular injections of insulin.

The drinking water supply is critically important for maintaining good health. If your dog's urine is dark yellow or orange and is produced in small quantities with a thick consistency, like syrup, he may not be getting enough fresh water, or he may be suffering from a urinary tract infection.

Watch your old dog's stool color and consistency for signs of incomplete digestion. Many older dogs eat well but lose weight because one organ or another (sometimes the pancreas) is no longer able to produce enough enzymes to digest his food. That problem can be corrected to some degree by mixing an enzyme supplement with the food. Additionally, you can grind the dry dog food, mix it with warm water (or, preferably, some no-calorie broth), or heat it a bit.

What are all those special diets I see at the vet's office?

If your Golden needs a special diet to help solve a dietary problem such as a food allergy, your veterinarian may suggest a particular dog food that contains ingredients such as lamb and rice, which are different from the ingredients in most dog foods. Another example is feeding your fat Golden a special low-calorie diet to help him reduce weight while giving him adequate nutrition. There are also prescription diets to help dogs with a variety of medical conditions, as I've just mentioned above.

Which dog food should I buy?

Nearly every dog owner and breeder has a different *favorite* brand of dog food. If you shop in a supermarket, you'll find one selection of brands, and if you buy from a pet supply store, you'll find another. Consumer preferences govern which brands will succeed and which ones will dry out in their bags while still on the shelf.

As an intelligent shopper, you should first look at the three dog food types and decide if you want to feed your Golden dry food, canned food or semimoist food. Then you must decide which brand you want. I'm going to assume you will choose a premium brand (your Golden deserves the best!), but there are dozens. So now you must compare the quality and quantity of nutrition contained in each bag or can, and you can only do that if you understand how to interpret the label, because all the premium brands seem to have similar ingredients. (You'll find information on how to read dog food labels on page 73.)

If several brands are very similar, the next step might surprise you. Ask a shelf stocker in the store which brands he replaces most frequently. You notice I didn't advise you to ask the manager which food is best? That's because she might be inclined to point you toward her most profitable product—not necessarily the most nutritious food. And the brands that are sold less frequently become stale after awhile and lose some of their nutritive value.

Then you should buy a *small* bag, or several cans, of your choice and give it a try. If your Golden eats it readily, it doesn't upset his digestive system or cause a lot of flatulence and it doesn't smell bad in the kitchen cabinet, you've probably found the food you want.

What are the differences between the types of dog foods?

Dry food or kibble is the least expensive and most commonly fed dog food in America. It's made from various animal and plant sources. Eggs, soy and cereal grains, artificial and natural flavors, colors and preservatives also are included. The palatability of dry foods (how tasty they are to eat) varies, and as you descend the ladder of quality and price, you'll find more plant products in the kibble and less palatability.

Canned foods contain more than 50 percent water—you read that right, you're buying 50 percent plain old water. Be sure to read the ingredient list of any canned food before you buy it. You may find that it's primarily made of soy products, and that real meat is very scarce in a product that looks quite meaty. Remember that canned food's nutritional content must be calculated by using the *dry* weight of its ingredients and not the gross weight of everything inside the can.

You can feed canned foods either alone or mixed with dry food of equal quality. If you buy canned food, never buy a cheap house brand to mix with a premium dry food. The former will dilute the nutritional value of the latter, and your dog will end up with a poor diet.

Semimoist foods are those little bags of meaty-looking chunks. Usually they're primarily soy and other plant products that have been flavored and loaded with sugar, preservatives and dye. They're dehydrated so that the manufacturers can sell them in bags. Some contain real meat in modest proportions, and all are very palatable. The problem with them is threefold. First, the preservatives may cause allergies and result in digestive upsets. Second, their dehydrated state requires a dog to consume large quantities of water after eating, and that may cause frequent urination and digestive upsets. Third, they are expensive relative to the amount of nutrition in the food.

So is canned food better or worse than kibble?

The packaging of the three different types of food is less important than the nutritive value and cost of each. For example, a particular canned food may contain the same nutritional elements as a dry food, but it could cost five times as much per pound because it's over half water and is packaged in small quantities.

Aren't all dog foods pretty much alike?

Not by a long shot! Dog food varies from pure junk at the lowest end of the price range to excellent premium food. Somewhere in between are the excellent canine foods, both premium and brand-name dry and canned products.

What if I feed my dog generic food?

The main difference between generic brands and name brands is that generic brand manufacturers often buy the least expensive ingredients from season to season. The grain, and therefore the quality of nutrition in the sack or can, varies from season to season. Those foods also may add fewer vitamin and mineral supplements than brand names and may use more preservatives or artificial flavorings.

Can't a mediocre dog food be souped up by adding vitamin and mineral supplements and meat scraps?

The short answer is "no." Dogs will eat just about anything imaginable, and your Golden will certainly eat the lousiest dry dog food you can find if you make it halfway palatable. But that's not what Golden ownership is all about. An unbalanced diet will affect every aspect of your dog's life, and will eventually catch up with his health.

Is that why my veterinarian says premium dog foods cost less than the cheaper brands?

Yes. The professional knows that excellent quality dog foods cost more to manufacture than cheap ones. She also knows that premium foods contain the best ingredients and are more thoroughly tested by feeding trials. Although the actual cash outlay is greater when buying a premium food, you actually feed your dog less of the better food because it is denser in nutrients. You veterinarian also believes the nutritional value compensates for the cost. If you go with a cheap dog food, you will certainly pay for your error in veterinary bills down the road.

How much will it cost a year to keep my Golden on a decent diet?

There are too many variables to calculate this figure accurately although you can expect to pay no less than $200 to $400 a year to feed your Golden. The cost of dog food is directly related to its quality, cost of production and the quantity demanded by your Golden. You can buy a modestly priced brand-name diet at the supermarket for about 35 cents per pound. Premium foods may cost twice that much. Normally, dogs eat more before they're two years old and less afterward. Neutered dogs usually demand less food than intact dogs.

How do I interpret dog food labels?

When you read a label, it may say the food is *complementary* or *complete*. You should feed complementary foods with another source of nutrients, but a complete diet can be your Golden's only source of food. Don't waste your time on complementary dog food.

Dry matter refers to the weight of the food after the water has been extracted.

Ingredients are listed in descending order of quantity, so if corn flour is listed as the first ingredient, there is more corn flour in the food than anything else. (By the way, if corn flour really is the first ingredient, put the bag back on the shelf!)

AAFCO regulates dog food labels and allows statements to be added to the label such as *complete and balanced*. When you see that statement on the label, along with something that says the food has undergone AAFCO feeding trials, it means it lacks no essential nutrients. If a product's label has no AAFCO statement, it doesn't mean that the food hasn't been formulated in accordance with feeding trials, but the only way you'll ever know is to call the company. Most dog foods have toll-free numbers listed on the package.

Bioavailability is very important. You may see the terms *total nutrients* or *digestible nutrients*, but they aren't the same as the *bioavailable* nutrient levels. The bioavailable level of an element is the amount of the element that's usable by the dog for energy. In other words, if a dog food label states that it contains a certain amount of protein, but doesn't specify what the bioavailability is, you should try another food. Plant products (soy and other cereal grains) may be high in protein, but dogs use plant protein poorly.

How often should I feed my Golden?

Your dog's breeder will tell you the established routine when you pick up your Golden puppy. After six months of age, you should feed him twice a day. After a year of age, he can get by on a single daily meal, but will be happier and healthier if you split his daily ration into two meals. During times of stress, such as when your dog is competing in canine sports, hunting, training, breeding and swimming, you should slightly increase his total daily ration and the frequency of meals.

What is free-choice feeding?

It means leaving dog food out all the time, so the dog can eat as much as he wants, whenever he wants. Of course, this will only work with dry dog food. Free-choice feeding may work for some breeds, or individuals of any breed, but it generally isn't recommended for Goldens because they're often gluttons. Instead, it's best to feed your Golden individual meals at specific times of the day.

How do I know if he's getting enough to eat?

Regardless of his age, when your Golden finishes a meal he should appear at least momentarily satisfied. If he immediately looks for more, you might consider giving him another small meal between regular feedings. Examine him no less than once a month, weigh him monthly (before a meal) and feel his ribs. If his ribs are prominent and he's at the low end of the desired weight for his age and height, you should increase the amount you are feeding him. Ask your veterinarian if you're in doubt about the dog's ideal weight.

I have another dog. Can they be fed together?

Competition for food may lead to overeating, fights, jealousy and other problems. It's best to feed them separately in different parts of the house, with doors closed between them. This precaution will prevent most problems and will enable you to control the amount of food each of your Goldens actually consumes. Always be sure both dishes are empty before you open the doors.

Are Goldens big eaters?

Absolutely! Let's face it—usually they're pigs. And, like some of their owners, they're snackers. They love to eat more than almost anything, so they're natural beggars. If you start out by feeding your Golden bites of junk food, pieces of your hamburger, a few French fries—in other words, increasing his diet when it should be stable—he'll become obese.

Lots of Goldens are fat. Is that dangerous?

Yes. Fat dogs aren't healthy dogs. If your dog grows beyond his normal dimensions, his life is at risk and that risk is compounded as he ages. Visible fat is deposited under the skin, and its weight adds to the stress on tendons, ligaments and joints. But what you can't see is the fat that's deposited in and around the body's organs, including your dog's muscles. Perhaps the greatest danger posed by too much fat is a heart muscle that's weakened by fatty infiltration, a liver that detoxifies poorly because of fat deposits within and surrounding it, or a pancreas that can't produce vital enzymes and hormones because of fat interference. Diabetes is known to occur more frequently in fat dogs, and arthritis signs are always worse in overweight Goldens.

Can I feed my Golden treats?

Of course, as long as they're low-calorie snacks. How could your Golden survive without them? Just remember that you should always count treats when adding up the total calories he eats, and the best treats are small biscuits, bite-sized pieces of jerky or cooked meat cubes taken from the fridge. Training treats enhance performance, and treats you give him just to be friendly are almost as important.

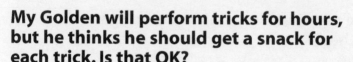

My Golden will perform tricks for hours, but he thinks he should get a snack for each trick. Is that OK?

Often amateur trainers forget that after you teach a dog something, you should gradually discontinue the food reward in favor of physical and verbal rewards, such as assuring him that he's a good dog and giving him a pat on the head. To continue giving him a treat for each performance will develop a nuisance behavior that you'll regret—and will make his training unreliable.

What kind of snacks should I give my Golden?

Some folks use peanut butter. A better choice is string beans. Read the caloric content on a can of string beans and compare it to the calories on a jar of peanut butter. You'll find the beans contain 20 calories per half cup. Natural peanut butter (without sugar) contains 200 calories per *ounce*. Sure, he'll probably prefer a nice dollop of peanut butter (who wouldn't), but which do you suppose is the best snack for a Golden who tends to be overweight?

Other snacks that are low in calories, but most Goldens like, are cooked carrots, raw celery, raw or cooked greens, asparagus, cucumbers and tomatoes. These foods yield about 20 (or less) calories per 100 grams. Beef bouillon or consommé are also low in calories, and you can use these for flavoring his snacks.

Can I give him a piece of chocolate as a treat?

Chocolate in any quantity is always bad for your dog. Chocolate is made from the cacao plant and contains the stimulant theobromine, which is toxic to dogs if they eat it in large quantities. Signs of chocolate poisoning are relative to the quantity and quality of the chocolate consumed. Early signs are panting, nervousness, vomiting and diarrhea. Later you may observe serious signs such as loss of urinary control, convulsions, coma and possibly death. You won't see any of those signs when your plucky Golden plucks an average size chocolate bar from the counter, but if she manages to scarf up a whole box of dark chocolate, it's an emergency.

Baking chocolate contains 400 mg per ounce of the toxin, and is the most dangerous. Dark chocolate is next most deadly, with 150 mg per ounce, and milk chocolate contains a mere 50 mg per ounce and is the least dangerous. To put that dosage in perspective, to risk death an 80-pound Golden would have to eat 40,000 mg of theobromine, which is slightly over six pounds of baking chocolate or 125 pounds of milk chocolate. Not likely! However, much smaller doses of chocolate can still make your dog very, very sick.

What should I do for chocolate poisoning?

If you bake with chocolate and your Golden gets into the chocolate bowl, rush her to the veterinarian. If that's impossible, induce vomiting or immediately give her activated charcoal to absorb the toxin. Administer 0.45 to 1.8 grams of activated charcoal in two to four ounces of water per pound of body weight, and dose her with this every two to four hours.

Can I feed my Golden table scraps?

Don't do it! Your Golden will unquestionably be happy to clean up everyone's plate and any leftovers that are in the fridge. You won't immediately notice the results of scrap feeding, but in a year or so, you'll be sorry! Over time, your dog's diet will be seriously unbalanced. He's also likely to put on weight.

If my food is good for me, why aren't scraps good for my Golden?

Sometimes people feed table scraps to lower the cost of feeding a Golden. Unfortunately, that plan amounts to formulating your dog's diet from a limited quality and quantity of human foods. You can't possibly provide him with a wholesome, healthful diet from your leftovers, and in reality you're teaching him to eat garbage instead of good, nutritious dog food. What you save in food bills you'll probably forfeit in veterinary bills.

Should I give my Golden leftover steak bones?

Absolutely not! Cooked bones splinter easily and can get stuck in your dog's throat or digestive tract. This applies to fish, poultry, beef, pork and lamb bones. However, you can safely allow your Golden to chew on a *raw* knucklebone, which is the joint end of a beef leg bone. Take it away and discard it when he has chewed on it for a few hours. Chewing on the raw cartilage and slick bone surface is good for his teeth, and he won't get many calories from it.

6

How Do I Groom a Golden Retriever?

What does grooming a Golden entail? • Why is grooming important? • What are the special characteristics of a Golden's coat? • What equipment do I need for grooming? • How much brushing and combing does my Golden need? • Do Goldens shed seasonally? • Does my Golden's hair need to be trimmed? • What are mats? • How often does my Golden need a bath? • Do I need to trim my Golden's nails? • Does a Golden need special ear care? • What if he has gunk in his eyes? • What are grass awns? • What are hotspots? • What about dental care? • Do anal sacs cause a problem in Goldens? • What are calluses?

What does grooming a Golden entail?

Grooming means personal care for your Golden's body. Regular brushing and combing are a big part of that, but grooming also involves many functions that aren't associated with combing and brushing. It includes regular inspection for parasites, ear cleanliness, dental attention, nail trimming and routine coat care.

Why is grooming important?

Regular grooming is the first line of preventive health. It may lead you to discover ailments you didn't even suspect your dog had.

Regular brushing keeps foreign objects and dirt out of the coat, keeps the skin and hair healthy, removes dead hair and stimulates the growth of new hair. Equally important, being groomed brings pleasure to your companion. Any time you touch your Golden buddy, you deepen the bond between your dog and yourself. When you spend time with him, even if you have a grooming tool in your hand, he'll love it because he'll learn that the time you devote to grooming is all his.

If you neglect your Golden's grooming, it will result in terrific stress on your vacuum cleaner and can damage your Golden's physical and mental health. At the very least, you will have a dirty, unkempt, matted dog—and this appearance will be distressing to both your dog and you.

What are the special characteristics of a Golden's coat?

Just as the color of a Golden can be anything from deep red to light wheat, the coat varies so much from dog to dog that it's really hard to say exactly what kind of coat a Golden has. In general, a Golden has a long, wavy, water-repellant topcoat that's a bit hard and stiff. Underneath is a softer, denser, insulating undercoat. But in fact, coats range from straight to curly, short to long, thin to thick.

Goldens with a soft, full undercoat (especially prevalent in neutered dogs and those on thyroid medication) will be more likely to develop mats and will need extra brushing. A heavy coat can mat within a week if you do not brush it frequently. A coat that's long and curly will also need extra attention, because it is more likely to mat and to trap debris. A short, curly coat is among the easiest to care for.

What equipment do I need for grooming?

You'll need:

- A pin brush (a brush with long, straight pins) or slicker brush (a brush with long wire pins that are bent at the end, set into a rubber head)
- A stainless steel grooming comb and a stainless steel flea comb
- A nail clipper made especially to cut the thick nails of dogs
- A pair of blunt-ended scissors
- A canine toothbrush, or finger cover or even a child's toothbrush and canine toothpaste, or at least a small towel you can use to wipe the teeth clean

You may also need:

- A grooming rake (it actually looks like a tiny garden rake and is good for pulling out lots of dead undercoat)
- A hand-held hair dryer (not absolutely necessary, but it is convenient)

How much brushing and combing does my Golden need?

His coat requires a quick brushing at least twice a week, with more thorough combing and brushing less frequently. Using your slicker brush, begin at the front of the dog and work your way back, being sure to thoroughly brush the neck and throat and behind the ears. Use a comb on the longer hair on the tail and legs, and underneath the ears. Make sure you remove all the tangles from his coat, especially in the longer leg, tail, chest and ear fringes.

Do Goldens shed seasonally?

Certainly, there are periods of heavier shedding. They may coincide with the change of seasons or (for a bitch) coming into and out of heat, or there may be other reasons. When your Golden is shedding heavily, the undercoat dies and becomes loose and you'll need to brush him more frequently. The best way to ensure that the new undercoat grows in lovely and healthy is to remove as much of the old undercoat as possible. You can do this by running your hands through the coat, rubbing the skin of the neck and shoulders, back, sides and rear legs. This will loosen the dead hair, which will then be easier to brush out. A grooming rake is also very useful for removing large amounts of dead undercoat in a single stroke. Don't be surprised if you end up with a pile of hair that is almost as big as your Golden!

Does my Golden's hair need to be trimmed?

Your Golden's coat is meant to be natural, and you won't need to trim him the way you might a long-haired breed like a Maltese or a curly-coated dog like a Poodle. However, a little trimming will help keep your dog neater and more comfortable.

Trimming the long hair around the feet will mean your dog will track less dirt into the house. The hair on the bottom of the foot is often cut so that it is even with the pads, so that the dog walks on his pads and not on his hair. This will help keep the hair between the toes from becoming matted, and keep foreign objects from lodging there.

If you find the area under the tail to be dirty, you may want to gently trim the hair around the tail and anus. You can do all of this trimming with scissors.

A hunter often trims down her Golden's long lower leg hair and the hair of his feet, tail and ears in the warm months to help keep ticks and grass seeds out of the coat, and that practice doesn't result in damage to the coat. Goldens often have skin problems (which may be hereditary), and those lesions need to be shaved and medicated, but that has nothing to do with the weather.

Should my Golden be shaved down in the summer?

No. Probably it won't hurt the Golden to lose his hair for a season, but it's completely unnecessary, and the new coat may emerge with a different texture, color and character.

What are mats?

Mats are loose hair that forms into tight clumps when a dog scratches or chews at an area more than normal, when an area is not properly groomed, or in areas that naturally rub against one another. As the mats become larger, they work their way closer to the skin and can become very painful as they pull and pinch at the skin.

Do mats form more often in some places than in others?

Absolutely. The longer fringe-like hair on the legs and tail (called *feathers*) tends to mat more easily, as do the hair in the armpits. Mats are also more likely to be found underneath the ears and between the toes and pads of the feet, especially if the dog tends to chew at his feet.

What's the easiest way to remove mats?

By attacking them before they become established. This means frequent combing and brushing. Don't wait until you can see and feel mats. If you catch a mat that has just started to form, you can sometimes brush or comb it out, or remove it with a mat splitter. But don't abuse your Golden's skin by digging and pulling at anything but the tiniest, loosest mat with the comb. Instead, use a pair of blunt-end scissors to split the mat into several shreds or to completely cut it from his coat. If you neglect a mat to the point where it is quite close to the skin (something you never should do!), it becomes risky to try to slip scissors between the mat and the skin. You'll need to take your dog to a professional groomer for a crew cut of the area. Believe me, the lost hair will grow back.

How often does my Golden need a bath?

When he's dirty, clean him up. Dogs in general, and Goldens in particular, don't need regular or frequent bathing. Bathing any dog with an undercoat is a big job that you shouldn't undertake more often than necessary. In addition, too much bathing will strip the natural oils from your dog's coat that give him protection from cold water and inclement weather.

Show dogs are bathed much more frequently—sometimes every week—but their owners use coat conditioners and other products to keep the dogs in good shape.

Do I need a special canine shampoo?

Yes, and get the best one you can find. Good canine shampoos clean the coat, condition it and replenish it with the essentials the washing may remove.

Never ever bathe your Golden with a detergent soap, your own shampoo or a shampoo that contains insecticides. Detergents and human shampoos remove natural oils from his coat and interfere with its ability to shed water, and insecticide shampoos often contain detergents with unneeded chemicals added.

Do I need to trim my Golden's nails?

An outdoor Golden who frequently runs in rough country or a city dog who runs a lot on rough concrete hardly ever needs a pedicure, but their indoor and backyard buddies often grow nails that need trimming regularly. The structure of the dog's feet and front end also affects nail care; dogs who are well put together overall need less nail care.

Check your dog's nails weekly, but don't cut them until needed. If you hear your dog's nails clicking on the floor, you need to cut them. Old dogs in particular require more frequent nail care.

What if I don't want to trim my dog's nails?

You'll have to make regular appointments with the vet or the dog groomer to have it done. Untrimmed nails can deform your dog's feet. As the nails get longer and longer, the toes spread out. The foot splays, and the feet no longer properly support the dog's weight. Very long nails can also grow back into the dog's pads, causing him enormous pain.

Less serious is the fact that long nails will scratch your floors, your furniture and you.

What's involved in trimming the nails?

Start with a very sharp nail clipper. Examine your Golden's toenail structure very carefully under a bright light. You'll see that the base of the nail is somewhat cylindrical, but as it nears the tip, the underside of the nail becomes hollow and V-shaped. If his nails are semi-transparent, you'll be able to see the blood vessels in the center of each. That bundle of blood vessels and nerves is called the *quick*, and you cut the nail beyond the quick. If his nails are dark and you can't see the quick, take only a small slice of nail with each snip. Never cut into the rounded portion.

What are dewclaws?

Dewclaws are the Golden's fifth toes, located above the feet on the inside of the wrists. Sometimes the dewclaws are removed while the puppy is tiny, but if not, be sure to trim them whenever you cut the other nails. Check the dewclaws once a week because they don't touch the ground and are therefore never worn away. Neglected dewclaw nails sometimes grow in complete circles and often penetrate into the toe pad.

Does a Golden need special ear care?

The Golden's ears are major objectives during a regular grooming session. The flaps that cover a Golden's ear canals help keep cold water out, but they also hold moisture and foreign bodies in—inviting infection. You should inspect the ears at least once a week for foul odors, excessive wax, foreign bodies such as grass awns or other weed seeds and tenderness or pain, and you should clean them if needed. Take your Golden to a veterinarian if you see copious dark brown or black wax, which is one sign of ear mites.

After your Golden has been swimming, or after a bath, it helps if you gently wipe the outer ear canals dry with a clean cotton ball.

What is involved in cleaning his ears?

You can wipe the outer ear clean with a small towel. Then gently lift the ear flap and look inside. First, look into the canals carefully with a magnifying glass and strong light. If you see an object such as an awn, and if you can reach it with a pair of tweezers, pull it gently from his ear canal. You can remove small visible wax deposits with a cotton-tipped swab that's been soaked with alcohol. You shouldn't poke at anything beyond the area that's plainly visible. If you can't see anything in the canal, but his ear is sore or smells bad, take him to his veterinarian. Your veterinarian can also show you how to use an ear-cleaning solution.

What if he has gunk in his eyes?

Normally, a small amount of white or clear mucus is found at the inside corners of his eyes. This is normal, but any more than that is reason for investigation. Some Goldens have very long hairs around the eyerim that turn in toward the eye. These can irritate the eye, and should be kept trimmed or can be removed by a vet.

Do check your dog's eyes regularly for foreign objects, and also check them anytime he is squinting or blinking, he shows any tenderness, his third eyelid is showing or there is a yellowish or greenish discharge. Usually, conjunctivitis or corneal ulcers are accompanied by a foul-smelling discharge. Foreign material such as dirt, seeds, pollens and the like will also cause a discharge, and you should wash them out immediately with artificial tears.

What are ulcerated corneas?

The cornea is the transparent front surface of the eyeball. A Golden, like any other bird dog, runs with his eyes wide open, and frequently a hunting dog suffers a serious problem when he's traveling through the tall grasses and weeds. Briars or plant leaves rub against his face and scratch the cornea of his eye. A grass seed or awn may also fall or migrate into his eye and scratch the cornea.

The nictitating membrane, or third eyelid, is a structure that's normally seen nicely folded in the inside corner of the eye, and is nothing more than a tiny pinkish mass. When your Golden runs through tall grass and weeds, the third eyelid spreads out, covers and protects most of the cornea. Sometimes a seed becomes trapped under this membrane, though, and is held tightly, where it rubs into the tender corneal tissue. The rubbing causes an erosion called an ulcer.

When you see any abnormal discharge from an eye, take your Golden to his veterinarian for examination and treatment.

What are grass awns?

These pesky little grass seeds are responsible for canine foot and ear infections in virtually every part of the country. The seeds are submarine-shaped; one end is sharp and pointed, and the other end is armed with a long, stickerlike beard. These little monsters jump out of the weeds to attack your socks and compel you to stop and pull them out. They also get caught in the hair of outdoor dogs like your Golden.

Awns' sharp points have no respect for intact skin and penetrate it with the greatest of ease. The seed's coating consists of a series of very stiff layers, like fish scales. When an awn penetrates your dog's skin, it continues to travel into the deeper tissues and sometimes emerges as high up the leg as the elbow. Often the afflicted Golden exhibits pain and lameness, and he licks at the awn, trying to remove it. It can cause lots of trouble if it penetrates a joint and causes infection there. Usually the awns emerge through the skin or migrate near the skin's surface, and can be retrieved with very minor surgery.

A hunting dog or one who is exercised in fields may pick up a little awn in the fringe hair of his ear. From there, the awn may travel up the ear into the ear canal and can cause loads of mischief when it reaches the lower limits of the canal. An awn is often the cause of infection in the lower ear canal, and occasionally one needs to be removed from the eardrum.

Grass awns are always trouble. If you exercise your Golden in areas where they're common, keep his ear flap hair clipped short and his toe hair trimmed as short as possible. This will prevent many of the serious problems that result from awn migration. Awns may collect in the hair of his body, and these can lead to chewing and licking, resulting in a hotspot.

What are hotspots?

Also called moist dermatitis or moist eczema, these skin lesions usually start as an allergic reaction to something like a flea bite or a grass awn. Your Golden licks and chews at the spot to stop the itching, and in doing so, the wet hair mats down. Bacteria from his skin grow rapidly in the warm, moist lesion, and he suddenly has a hotspot. The lesion spreads, and it's possible for it to encompass several inches or a foot in a very short time. Because Goldens are prone to skin allergies, they are also prone to hotspots.

Are hotspots curable?

One of the Golden Retriever's worst enemies is hotspots. A hotspot is painfully irritating to the affected Golden, and is also a headache to the veterinarian who treats him. Don't procrastinate in taking your dog to the vet, or you'll be sorry! Some dogs' hotspots are emergencies because they spread so quickly and irritate the dog to the point of self-destruction. To delay treatment can compromise the Golden's general mental and physical health.

Treatment includes shaving the hair from the entire lesion and the surrounding skin for an inch or two in every direction. This will allow air to reach the lesion to dry it. You must also stop the Golden's licking. This includes physical prevention and possibly tranquilizers or oral or injectable steroids. Topical medications are usually part of the treatment package, as well.

Hotspots are never easy to treat, but prompt and careful attention does work.

What about dental care?

Veterinarians advise regular tooth brushing to prevent the buildup of tartar, gum disease, periodontal disease and bad breath. You should brush your Golden's teeth every day, or at least once a week. It takes very little time, and you can do it easily using either a finger cover or canine toothbrush and doggy toothpaste. Don't use human toothpaste because dogs cannot rinse and spit—canine toothpaste is formulated to be swallowed. The bristles on human toothbrushes are usually too stiff for a dog. Many people believe that chewing on a dog biscuit or two each day is sufficient, but it rarely works very well and isn't nearly as effective as using a brush and doggy toothpaste every day.

Do his teeth need scaling by a veterinary dentist?

Some dogs do. Check your dog's mouth regularly, and if you notice an offensive odor, a swollen or inflamed area or a buildup of tartar, take your dog to the vet.

Do dogs ever need fillings or extractions?

Your dog's dental health should be included in her regular veterinary examinations. Young Goldens usually have few dental problems, but senior Goldens are subject to tartar, loose or broken teeth and abscesses. Usually cavities aren't a problem, but they're possible, and your veterinarian or a canine dentist can treat them. Extractions are more likely to be necessary in rescued Goldens whose dental health has been neglected.

Do anal sacs cause a problem in Goldens?

Anal sacs are the pair of small, hollow structures under the skin on either side of his anus. When they are full, you can feel them with your fingers, and they normally drain though two tiny tubes or pores that open through the sphincter muscle, which encircles his anus. These sacs normally fill with a foul, oily fluid, and empty with each bowel movement. If the openings become clogged, they cause distress. You'll know your dog has a problem because he will scoot his behind along the ground, and may also bite at it. If you see this behavior, your dog needs to see a veterinarian, because the anal sacs can become painful and infected. If your dog is prone to this problem, the vet can show you how to empty the anal sacs yourself.

What are calluses?

A callus represents a pressure point on your Golden's body. Usually it occurs on his elbow, on the outside of his foot or over his hipbone. Those areas are abused when a senior Golden repeatedly rests his body on hard surfaces. The hair wears away and the skin becomes a thick, wrinkled callus that occasionally becomes infected. Preventive care includes rubbing a softening lotion into these calluses, but a better plan is to pad his napping places to prevent calluses from forming.

7

What's Involved in Training a Golden Retriever?

How easy is it to train a Golden Retriever? • What is *trainability*? • Why is it important to train my Golden? • What training does my Golden need to be a well-behaved pet? • How much time will I have to spend training my Golden Retriever? • What will happen to my Golden's behavior if I don't have time to train him regularly? • Do I need to hire a professional trainer? • Do I need to join a training class? • What is special about training a Golden? • What principles should I remember when I begin training my dog? • What is dominance training? • What is compulsion training? • What equipment do I need to train my Golden? • What about crates and ex-pens? • What's the best way to housebreak my Golden pup? • What is the Canine Good Citizen program? • Can I train my Golden to assist me with a disability? • What are therapy dogs?

How easy is it to train a Golden Retriever?

Goldens are very trainable dogs who bond well with their owners and focus on them most of the time. They are very bright and patient with amateur trainers. Generally, a Golden is a willing student if the teacher is equally bright and patient, but the trainer must treat the canine student with respect and conduct the lessons with consistency and in small doses. Build a tight bond with him while he's a puppy, and as an adult he'll listen, focus and perform tasks without dispute. In exchange, he'll expect nothing more or less from you than approval and verbal praise.

Some Goldens are a bit lazy and more difficult to train, but rarely are they stubborn or intractable, and most Goldens easily understand a competent trainer's instructions. A few are very quickly trained and well mannered and never make a mistake, but they aren't the majority. Most Goldens require clear instruction and considerable training to be perfect pets.

What is *trainability*?

Trainability is a relative term, but generally, it's the capacity and desire to be taught to do various tasks. It includes inherent intelligence, the ability to learn by example, and a desire to win the approval of the trainer. A highly trainable dog fixes his focus on his handler at every moment and tries always to understand exactly what she wants with each signal. Trainability isn't a consistent feature of every intelligent breed, but it's a strong reason for the Golden Retriever's popularity.

Often the most trainable dog is the one who bonds tightly with his handler; this dog will try to do virtually anything he is asked. Sometimes a Golden doesn't transfer this trainability from one person to another, but more often, he will perform for anyone in the family.

Is a Golden more trainable than some other breeds?

The answer is yes. The desire to please, which Goldens possess so strongly, is a big part of trainability. In addition, this soft, beautiful, tough but gentle friend is quite intelligent. I suppose someday we'll be able to legitimately evaluate the I.Q. of dogs (and that may be a shock to our pre-conceived notions). We do know that some breeds are more clever than others. Typical Goldens reason clearly, make decisions quickly, solve problems easily and display their intelligence regularly. These canine attributes are chiefly individual characteristics that can't be categorized by breed.

Why is it important to train my Golden?

Your dog is born with a set of instincts that guide him on how to live in canine society in the natural world. But he lives in human society in our world, and he hasn't a clue how to cope. Dogs who are untrained simply do what comes naturally—barking, nipping, biting, chewing, jumping on, urinating and defecating on what they want, where they want, when they want. Such a dog is a nightmare to live with, but you can't blame him for being a dog.

Good manners make your dog priceless. A well-mannered dog is accepted and appreciated by everyone in your community. Manners dictate his behavior and his responses to the human environment. For example, when you've finished playing and tell him to *settle*, he finds a spot where he can see everyone and he camps there. When you speak to him, he looks at you and waits for your next instruction.

Dogs also naturally live in packs, and look to a pack leader to make decisions for them. Training your dog teaches him that you are the leader. If you do not teach him this important lesson, he will have no leader to look up to, and can become nervous, anxious and unpredictable.

I want to enjoy my Golden. Can't I just play with him and hope for the best?

Play is actually one of the best training tools a smart dog trainer uses. Play is any activity your dog really enjoys, and Goldens will delight in all diversions that bring you into the picture. He'll perceive your training as just another game—unless you bore him by dragging your sessions on for hours or making them very repetitive. He'll learn what you desire without realizing that he's being trained. It's up to you to direct his play toward functional, practical ventures.

What training does my Golden need to be a well-behaved pet?

You should begin with housebreaking, some simple obedience commands (such as sit, stay, come and heel), some human and canine socialization lessons, and some dominance training (see page 98). Training to pass the Canine Good Citizen test (see page 104) is an excellent goal, and if your Golden passes this test, you will certainly have a well-mannered pet. But that isn't the place to stop. Goldens are so smart and so trainable, the sky's the limit!

How much time will I have to spend training my Golden Retriever?

A lifetime! If you're lucky, your Golden will never graduate and will always be a willing student. He'll appreciate every minute you spend with him, whether it's for specific short training sessions or long walks in the park. While he's young, allocate 10 or 15 minutes two or three times a day for training. After he has learned his lessons, enjoy your time together—all you can possibly spare—learning new things, and both you and he will reap many rewards.

What will happen to my Golden's behavior if I don't have time to train him regularly?

No one appreciates an undisciplined dog, and poor manners are directly proportional to a dog's size. So a big Golden with no training is a bigger annoyance than a small dog with no training. Your undisciplined Golden won't understand why everyone is shunning him, and you'll be embarrassed and unwelcome at canine-human gatherings. Quite possibly, you'll become one of the dog owners who are dissatisfied with your pet, and another beautiful Golden Retriever will end up in a rescue shelter.

Why should I train my puppy to stop jumping up?

Because one of these days, he'll weigh 75 pounds and will be a solidly built, powerful dog. He'll topple kids and even knock down adults. Play can get out of hand, too, and aggressive puppies become aggressive adults. Better to stop this horrible habit before it begins.

How do I stop his habit of jumping up?

First, ask yourself, "Why does he jump up?" Because he wants to greet you. And to do this properly, he must reach your face with his tongue. Altering this behavior should start as early as the habit begins, usually when your Golden is still a tiny pup.

You need the aid of a few children about six or eight years old, and they should be great actors. (Show me a kid that age, and I'll show you a great actor!) The acting begins when the pup and kids are all in the backyard playing. Each time the puppy jumps up on a child, the child should pretend to be knocked over and begin to cry. The kid shouldn't scold or swat the pup, but instead, totally ignore him, slowly get up and walk away from him. The child's acting will seriously impress the pup, and by the time he's knocked over every child and witnessed their dismay, he'll probably be cured of this vice. Sometimes several sessions are needed, but it will work!

You can also do this without kids. Call your pup to you at unexpected times, and each time he arrives in front of you, tell him to sit. Then kneel down and allow him to lick your face. Then stand, quickly turn and walk away. Soon he'll get the idea that face licking as a greeting is OK, but it must be done with decorum and never in a frenzy.

Do I need to hire a professional trainer?

Having the help and advice of a professional trainer will undoubtedly enhance your Golden's tutoring and make the process much smoother and perhaps quicker. However, training strengthens the bond between a dog and his handler, and is a great confidence builder for your Golden. Hiring a trainer for your companion's routine education means you'll lose half the joy of the relationship with your fun-loving pooch.

If you are really struggling to train your dog, though, or if your dog shows even the slightest signs of aggression, a professional trainer is a must.

If I want to hire a pro, how do I find one?

If you're looking for a trainer to help you teach your dog overall good manners, ask at your veterinarian's office, your local humane society, your dog's breeder and your local dog club for referrals. If you have neighbors who have particularly well-trained dogs, you can also ask them. If you're interested in trainers who specialize in hunting dogs, obedience or show training, agility, freestyle dancing or other advanced training, contact a club that sponsors these activities. Clubs often have training groups that you can join.

Do I need to join a training class?

Kindergarten classes that teach canine socialization are nearly essential for all puppies. Humane societies, dog clubs and private training schools all offer these types of classes. You may also find there are classes in your local park or community center. Ask for referrals at all the same places where you'd ask about a private trainer (see above).

What is special about training a Golden?

Uppermost in your mind should be the fact that Goldens are *soft*, which means they don't respond well to harsh training methods. He wants to please you, but he can't understand what you want unless you *show* him. Train him first to listen to your voice, to watch you, your hands, your signals, and he'll succeed. If he focuses on tiny tasks and does them well, that's probably an indication that he'll grasp more complex training more quickly. Never lose your patience when training your Golden. You must keep your composure and display great patience and consistency, calm and tolerance. Keep your instructions short and to the point, and never teach your dog something that conflicts with what you've already taught. Never let him become bored by ritual, and above all, keep your sense of humor.

What principles should I remember when I begin training my dog?

Consider his age. He isn't able to start college courses before he's been to elementary school. Evaluate his experience. If he's watched other dogs do a task, he'll have a better idea of what is expected of him. Try the following precepts, and you'll succeed.

- **Be patient.** Never start a training session when you're in a hurry. Patience also means your ability to understand your Golden's intelligence and experience level, and train him accordingly. With patience, all things are possible. If either teacher or student becomes bored, take a break. Because if you persist, failure will follow.

- **Have brief sessions.** Never spend more than 5 or 10 minutes training a single task. When he's eight weeks old, repeat the task three times, reward him when he performs correctly and ignore him when he fails. Then call recess for the day and begin again tomorrow.

- **Maintain a balance.** Combine work sessions with play sessions and never ever expect his attention span to match yours. When he has performed a task *correctly* twice in succession, quit or play for awhile and then pick up the training with another task.

- **Be consistent.** Before you teach the first lesson, decide just how you will approach it and use the same command for the same action every time. Consistency is the most difficult principle for a trainer to learn, unless you've had prior teaching experience.

- **Know your dog's abilities and limitations.** Never underestimate your Golden's reasoning ability, but don't expect miracles. Be realistic. Never ask him to jump over a bar that's obviously too high for his size and maturity. Don't be surprised if he ducks under the bar, which quickly teaches him that there are two ways to get to the other side. Never ask him to tackle an undoable task, because it may cause irrevocable harm. He may try, fail, become discouraged, and that can defeat your training expectations.

- **Give short commands.** Understand your Golden's communication abilities. Give him short commands, never detailed ones. Your best intentions are lost in verbosity. Speak his name and follow with "down," not "lie down." Say "fetch," never "fetch the ball."

- **Learn how to communicate.** Observe your Golden's body language and attitude. Train yourself to recognize and differentiate his postures and facial expressions. From those signals you'll be able to tell when he understands what you're teaching. When his tail begins to wag with purpose, his ears perk and his attitude says, "Sure, I can do that," you'll know you're both on the right road.

- **Give rewards.** You should always applaud your Golden for success and routinely ignore his failures. Food treats are fine in the beginning, but taper them off later and replace them with verbal and physical rewards. A pat on the head, a scratch behind the ears and lots of praise will do quite nicely.

- **End on a positive.** Never end a training session negatively. For instance, if he doesn't understand what you want when you're teaching "stay," after a few unrewarded attempts, ask him to do something he already knows—perhaps sit. Then reward him for sitting and call recess. Always wait until the next day before trying to teach a task your dog has failed at. Consider what you were doing when he didn't catch on, and think of a new way to teach the command. Consult a trainer or another training book for a new idea.

- **Almost right is still wrong.** Don't reward a task that's attempted but not performed correctly. Ignore his failure, and if he fails again, give him another task that he can perform to perfection, then reward him and take him for a walk. Put the session on hold for a day or two, then try again.

- **Don't repeat a command.** He hears better than you do. He knows what you said, and may even understand what you want from him. If he refuses to comply, either enforce the command or give him something else to do, or wait a day and try again. If you hear yourself repeating the commands, ask yourself if you're boring or tiring your student.

- **Never give a command that you can't enforce.** Say he's a puppy and is standing four feet in front of you. You tell him "sit" and he hears, understands, but considers it unnecessary to obey. Don't lose your temper—you are the one who wasn't thinking. You can't reach out and gently press his bottom to the floor to enforce the command when he's four feet away, so it's your mistake.

- **Maintain your sense of humor.** A Golden is often quite clownish and may respond to a command in a unique manner that he has just invented. You might like his response better than the one you expected.

- **Never punish your Golden.** Punishment means meting out something negative in an attempt to correct an error. It doesn't work. Your dog doesn't realize what error he's made, and your punishment will simply cause him to wonder why you've suddenly changed your attitude. If you punish him, he will eventually become apathetic about your training attempts.

- **Never try to reason or negotiate with your Golden.** He can reason and you can reason, but your reasoning power is at a much higher level than his. If you find that he's totally unresponsive to your command, rethink the task and your approach. Try to find another way to present the task. He'll appreciate your effort, and you'll learn more about training your Golden.

- **Time his training sessions to take advantage of his attention.** If you're still using food rewards, present the training session shortly before mealtime. Goldens are always anxious to please, but when they expect food in their future, they're more attentive.

- **Teach by association.** In other words, associate the task to be learned with something the dog knows is pleasant. For example, a leash means that he's about to go for a walk. That means his favorite person will be accompanying him, and that's what he wants, so he looks forward to being on the leash.

- **Be certain he understands that you're the teacher and he's the student.** Role reversal often occurs with a smart dog like a Golden, and he ends up training you. After collar and leash training is well under way, take him on leash for a quick walk around the yard before you start training. He'll behave because the collar and leash have taught him at least two things: first, that this is a participation program, not a demonstration; and second, that you're holding the leash and he's at a little disadvantage because the collar's around his neck.

What is associative learning?

It's learning that relates the dog's action to the handler's reaction. For example, your Golden sits at your feet and you pet him. He *associates* his action (sitting) with your reaction (petting), and he repeats it each time he wants your attention. Maybe your Golden brings a ball to you and you toss it. He fetches it, brings it back and drops it at your feet, and so forth. (Guess who is training whom?) His innate desire to involve you in his game and to please you is reinforced by your kindness and consistency. That increases your bond and enhances his trainability.

What is dominance training?

This training is designed to help your Golden understand that you are the leader of his pack, regardless of his personality and temperament. It begins when he's a puppy and continues throughout his life. It's a fine idea, even if you know all about the wonderfully receptive and mild-mannered Golden Retriever, because it helps you maintain control over your Golden.

Dominance training actually is a continuation of the pack training he learned from his dam and siblings. There are several facets to this training that can be initiated at any age. However, with older dogs, especially a rescued dog about whom you have very little information, it's critically important to move slowly and deliberately, and never be in a hurry. As you'll notice, I have discussed some of these procedures in other chapters. Here's what you do.

- Nudge or tell him to move out of your way when you walk from room to room and he's lying in the doorway.
- Feed him after your family is finished and never tolerate begging for food.
- When you come home, ignore him for a period of time but give him plenty of attention later.
- Keep some of his toys out of reach, and when you give him one, put another one away.
- Don't allow him on your bed.
- Sit on the floor and invite him to lie alongside you. Handle his feet and toes and flex his leg joints.
- Pick up each ear and smell his ear canals.
- Open his mouth and examine his tongue, gums and teeth.
- Turn him on his back and rub his belly, chest, neck and tail.

If your Golden willingly accepts these procedures, he's a typical Golden and you can rest assured that he's under your control, regardless of his obedience to commands.

What is compulsion training?

This term (which has also been called "force" training) is misunderstood by nearly everyone, but it really isn't what it sounds like. It's teaching your Golden to obey and submit to your instructions when the requested task isn't instinctive to him. Does this sound awful? It's not! Sitting on command is not instinctive to any dog and is a learned behavior. When you teach your Golden to sit, that's actually compulsion training because you've taught your dog to do something that's not instinctive. Walking on a leash is another compulsion training exercise. When you rub his feet or massage his legs, that is another type of compulsion training that has a very useful purpose, because it ensures that you'll always be able to trim his toenails.

What equipment do I need to train my Golden?

For a puppy, a lightweight nylon leash and buckle collar is fine. You should remove the collar from the puppy when you aren't with him, until he has become accustomed to wearing it in your presence.

Use a training collar if you've adopted a rescue dog and aren't sure of his obedience, or in any case when you need a little more control on an adult dog. If you're doing obedience training, or if your Golden is a bit headstrong and you need more influence than a buckle collar, a training collar is better and is required by many obedience trainers for their classes. Chain training collars are OK for training your Golden, but they aren't any better than nylon training collars and the chain certainly wears off the hair around the dog's neck.

Never use a prong collar (sometimes called a pinch collar) on your Golden. If he's so difficult to handle because of his size or your weight, use a head halter (see page 100), not a prong collar.

A harness is of very little value when training, because the Golden can ignore your commands and you can't control him or influence him in any way while he's wearing one. A harness may work fine for well-trained and obedient Goldens, but during training you must maintain more control than it affords.

What is a training collar?

Formerly called a *choke* collar (definitely a misnomer!), this restraining collar can be made of leather, nylon or chain with a ring fastened at both ends. You drop the fabric or chain through one ring and attach the leash to the other ring, forming a collar that quickly tightens — and just as quickly loosens — with a tug. Place the collar on the Golden's neck so the leash end goes up his left side and crosses from his left to right over the top of his neck. You take your place on his right. When you tighten the leash, you are applying pressure to the dog's neck, and when you release it, the pressure is instantly released.

What is a head halter?

If you're experiencing difficulty controlling your Golden, buy a head halter at the neighborhood pet supply store. This device works on the same principle as a horse's halter, and buckles over the dog's muzzle as well as around his neck. When you take up slack from the leash, you apply no pressure to his neck, but his head is turned to the side. The head halter has proven extremely useful in controlling rambunctious terriers and aggressive big dogs, but you *rarely* need it on a mild-mannered Golden.

What about crates and ex-pens?

Some type of confinement within the house is necessary to housebreak a young puppy and keep him out of trouble, and that's what crates and ex-pens are for. A crate is a large cagelike enclosure, usually made of heavy wire or molded fiberglass. It makes an excellent confinement area for your Golden pup. His short stay in the crate usually doesn't require food and water, and if it does, most crates can be fitted with spill-proof dishes.

You can use a crate for your dog in motel rooms, homes of people with allergies, homes where disagreeable dogs reside and sometimes in the backseat of your car. A Golden pup often needs a secure place for time-outs when he becomes overly excited with playing children. The crate is invaluable for protection of the tiny pup when neighborhood children invade your household and he needs a bit of rest. Remember that your Golden's unbridled exercise can be very detrimental to his normal bone and joint development. When you buy a crate, choose a large or extra large size. Your eight-week-old puppy won't use the extra space, but he'll need it as an adult.

An ex-pen is an expandable, foldable, lightweight stainless steel "corral" that can be easily moved from place to place. It's made from heavy wire mesh and can be made bigger or smaller to fit your circumstances. It can be moved to the backyard if you have reason to confine your Golden to a small space there.

You can use either type of confinement as sleeping quarters for your young Golden puppy, and to keep him out of trouble when you can't be with him during the day.

What is crate training?

Crate training simply means accustoming your pup to being in his crate, using his blanket, a treat and some chew toys. Usually, a Golden adapts to crate training with ease, but you should use the crate (or ex-pen) regularly and always positively reinforce good crate behavior with a treat, toy or chewy. A smart owner will teach her puppy to sleep in the crate when he's very young so he doesn't resent it later.

How long can a dog stay in a crate?

The answer to this question depends on the age of the Golden, what quantities of liquid you allow him to drink before crating, the stage of housebreaking, the attitude of the dog and so forth. When you're just beginning to housebreak a pup, it's best not to rely on his bladder control for more than three or four hours. As he matures and starts paying attention to your routine, he will gradually learn to empty out before crating, and then you can leave him longer. However, the crate should never become an instrument of boredom and anxiety—no dog should ever be asked to spend the majority of his day in a crate.

You can leave an average adult dog in a crate overnight (seven to eight hours) with minimal problems. Puppies 8 to 12 weeks of age shouldn't be confined for more than four hours at a stretch during the night. You can take them out to the toilet area after four hours and return them to the crate for the rest of the night. Adolescents and most pups older than three or four months can stay in the crate overnight if they have no water two hours before bedtime and they have been taken out for a walk immediately before crating.

Don't expect any dog to stay content in a crate during the daytime for more than four to six hours. They *can* hold their eliminations longer than that, but crating for longer periods of time is nothing less than neglect on the owners' part. If you work outside your home, have a friend or relative take your dog out in the middle of the day, whether he's an older pup or an adult.

What's the best way to housebreak my Golden pup?

Your puppy was born with the instinct not to soil his nest. When he had to go, he instinctively crawled a short distance from his nest and that place was used as a toilet area. Thereafter, he instinctively chose to return to the same place because the odors attracted him there. That's normal dog behavior, and if he lived only with other dogs, it would be quite appropriate.

You must capitalize on your pup's instinct to move away from his sleeping spot, and teach your pup to meet a higher, human behavioral standard. And that means going outside in a particular spot. When you attempt to alter his instinctive habits, you must be patient, persistent and consistent. He'll quickly adopt your new standard of behavior because instinctively he wants to leave his eliminations away from his den, and all you need to do is direct and control this habit.

Choose a specific place outdoors, in a remote spot of the backyard that you can easily clean up, and there, in that toilet area, you should begin the training. Take him to the toilet area several times the very first day he's in your home, and take him every time that he begins nosing around in circles and acting as if he's looking for a place to eliminate. Take him there soon after every meal, as well.

Don't give him any food or water for two hours before bedtime. Take him for a walk around the backyard immediately before going to bed, stopping at the toilet area. Allow him to nose around for several minutes, and if he defecates or urinates, tell him how proud you are and scratch his ears abundantly.

Return him to the toilet area first thing every morning, after every meal and last thing each night. When he cries during the night, pluck him from his crate, carry him to the toilet area and wait there until he performs.

If he doesn't do anything in a few minutes, pick him up and carry him back to his crate.

Your consistency is critical. For the first week or so, never allow him out of your sight. If you leave the house, put him in the ex-pen or crate.

Never, ever scold or reprimand him for messing on the floor. He will have no idea what you are scolding him for, and will simply learn to fear you. If you catch him in the act, pick him up without comment and carry him to the toilet area, place him on the ground, and wait until he finishes. There's no need to show him what he has done because it was perfectly natural for him to urinate or defecate, but he hasn't yet discovered the proper spot to deposit it.

Clean the floor or carpet with appropriate cleaners and when you are finished, deodorize the area with a commercially available product sold for that purpose. Don't use ammonia products because they smell like urine as they evaporate. If possible, move his food and water dishes to that spot or cover it with his blanket. His normal response is to not use a feeding or sleeping place for eliminations. Then program *your* brain to get him outside more frequently.

I live in an apartment. Any suggestions?

Your life may be a bit more complicated, but if you're determined, you can handle it. For housebreaking, you'll need to take him to the street. There, he must urinate and defecate in the gutter and you're responsible for cleaning it up. Use the same technique, the same equipment and the same praise rewards as described above.

What about paper-training my puppy?

Paper-training works well for an apartment dog, but the technique doesn't teach him where you really want him to go, which is outside. Still, if you want to paper-train your pup, confine him in the ex-pen. Place his blanket, food and water dishes at one end, and cover the entire rest of the floor of the pen with several layers of newspapers. He will defecate and urinate on the papers because they are a distance from his food and bed. After a week or so, you can remove the pen but maintain the papers in the same place and he'll return to the papers for eliminations.

What is the Canine Good Citizen program?

It's the ultimate proof of good social manners. Canine Good Citizens prove they can successfully perform 10 specific tasks that are the basics of what every well-behaved dog should know. The dog simply passes or fails, and no score is given. If he fails, he can practice and take the test again. The test is provided by members of an AKC club under the rules of the AKC, but dogs of every description are allowed to participate, whether or not their heritage is known. Tests are discussed individually below, but if you're interested you should contact your Golden Retriever club and ask if they have a class. The various tests are much more easily taught in a class. If you want your very own copy of the AKC rules, you can download them from the web at www.akc.org.

Can I train my Golden to assist me with a disability?

Your decision to acquire a Golden might be based upon your need for assistance in your everyday life. Your Golden needs very little specific training to become an assistance dog for you. Untold numbers of disabled people use these dogs, called service dogs, every day. If you are incapacitated in any way, your Golden can be your companion and serve your needs as well. A Golden's main joy comes from being with you and pleasing you. If you live alone, you're bound to appreciate her help, but you'll benefit nearly as much from her companionship.

If you are wheelchair bound, bedridden or confined to a walker or crutches, your Golden can help in many ways after some simple obedience training. With a little effort and knowledge you can teach her to fetch your newspaper, bring you a magazine from a stand across the room, pick up the eyeglasses you dropped or find your lost comb. You can build her vocabulary and teach her the meaning of shoe, sock, hat, coat, blanket, keys, remote and so forth.

You can teach your faithful Golden to respond to emergencies such as fire, smoke or accident by barking an alarm for the neighbors to hear. This will relieve your human caregiver of some of the day-to-day chores, and the entire family, including the Golden, will appreciate his important role.

If you have significant hearing impairment, you might want to investigate training your companion to be a hearing assistance dog. Hearing assistance dogs learn to listen for specific sounds and respond to them in specific ways. If your Golden hears the phone ring, she'll alert you to that sound by leading you to the phone. If she hears a smoke alarm, she'll respond in a different manner. You can teach her to take you to the nursery when the baby cries, or take you to the door when someone knocks or the doorbell rings. The cooking timer or another alarm will cause her to respond according to her training. Consult your local Golden club secretary for the names of various nonprofit organizations that will help you with the training.

What are therapy dogs?

A therapy dog brings happiness and solace to people of all ages who cannot get out to be with dogs. They visit hospitals and nursing homes, schools and prisons. Seniors and physically or mentally compromised individuals benefit greatly from the happy face of a Golden Retriever, and the experience will boost your spirits as well. And you'll be surprised at how quickly a Golden adapts to these visits. Some therapy organizations' members visit schools, scout meetings, and other events as well as hospitals and nursing homes. They introduce their mild-mannered dogs to people in nearly every walk of life. The Golden Retriever is one of the best therapy dogs imaginable.

How can I learn more about therapy dogs?

Any dog involved in therapy work needs some basic training, and you should have him certified through a national or local therapy dog organization. The Delta Society is an international resource for therapy dogs. It has established screening programs for these dogs, and publishes newsletters and home study courses for volunteers. You'll find contact information in the Resources section at the end of this book.

8

What Kind of Exercise Does a Golden Retriever Need?

Do Golden Retrievers generally require a lot of exercise? • How much exercise does a Golden puppy need? • At what stage can I exercise my puppy outside the yard? • How much exercise should a young adult get? • How does exercise affect my Golden's physical development? • Does a senior Golden require much exercise? • What can happen if my Golden doesn't get the exercise she needs? • Can I let my dog run free during the day? • What if I don't have a fenced-in yard? • What's the best backyard exercise for a dog? • How can I exercise my Golden without a fenced yard? • How do I exercise my Golden's mind? • What if I want to get involved in tracking trials? • What about hunting with my dog? • What other canine sports can my Golden and I can participate in?

Do Golden Retrievers generally require a lot of exercise?

All dogs need exercise for the normal development of their bodies and minds. Sporting breeds with a racy appearance, like the German Short-haired Pointer and English Setter, have loads of energy and require great amounts of exercise. The Golden Retriever is mellower; she loves to play but conserves her energy, and would just as soon take a nap when the day's work is completed.

A Golden usually isn't hyperactive at any stage of life, but she has plenty of reserve energy. Your Golden won't demand excessive exercise, but her need for human interaction is considerable, and that need is extremely important to her mental and physical stability. Perhaps the Golden Retriever's Bloodhound heritage influences her moderate exercise requirements. As an adult, she'll work hard every day if you ask her to, but she likes her creature comforts when it's quitting time.

How much exercise does a Golden puppy need?

Modest exercise is sufficient, and because of her rapid growth rate, you should carefully monitor her exercise level. A few tennis ball tosses, a game of hide-and-seek or a little leash training is all your Golden puppy requires in one play session. Repeat this program two or three times a day. As an adolescent, she'll be more ambitious and can handle more exercise, but even then, you should curtail strenuous exercise until she has reached maturity.

Is there such a thing as too much exercise for a puppy?

Yes! Because Goldens are rather large dogs, they mature fairly slowly. Excessive exercise or too much weight can irreparably damage immature Goldens' bones and joints. If you have children who like to play with her, you must watch your young Golden's exercise closely to make sure she doesn't become fatigued, especially when she's very young. Active children often have greater endurance than a Golden puppy, but she won't give up.

At what stage can I exercise my puppy outside the yard?

Yard exercise is always best until she has mastered walking on a leash. That usually coincides with the completion of her first few vaccinations, at about three months old. At that time she'll be ready to go and can safely take walks around the neighborhood. If you're ready, you can enroll her in a puppy kindergarten class as well. She'll get plenty of exercise there.

Is it OK to exercise my Golden pup off leash if she minds fairly well?

That's not a good idea until your Golden has been vaccinated and is well-socialized with other dogs, and then only if you live in an area where dog parks are fenced and monitored. In such an enclosure, you can safely allow a well-socialized Golden off leash to cavort about. But your affectionate Golden probably will prefer your company. She's more apt to stay right beside you most of the time, leaving the cavorting to setters and terriers.

How much exercise should a young adult get?

A Golden yearling can handle long walks on lead and games of Frisbee, and can begin training for a canine competition sport, if you're willing. Obedience training also involves exercise that's good for her. She's ready for retriever training, swimming and about anything you and she are interested in, except for field work or carrying a pack. Wait until she is at least 18 months old to start those activities.

How does exercise affect my Golden's physical development?

The Golden is a medium-size dog with a sturdy, heavy body. Large bodies predispose dogs to developmental problems, which are triggered by excessive exercise and being overweight. Those problems occur because your Golden's skeletal and joint development lag behind her body development and her ambition. Her diet supplies what she needs to produce sound joints, but excess weight can apply stress to the forming cartilage, ligaments and tendons. Pain will result from that unintentional abuse of the *epiphyseal plates* of her long bones (the ends of a long bone, which are at first separated from the main bone by cartilage, before the end plate fuses to the main bone shaft), ligaments and tendons. Repeated trips to the veterinarian to diagnose and treat that pain can be disastrous to your dog's happiness and your veterinary budget.

Goldens are people oriented, and they're easily led into trouble because they don't think for themselves when they're young and ambitious. You, as an informed owner, must guard against those developmental problems.

The information here about exercise is a generalization that fits the breed, but you should ask a veterinarian or an experienced Golden Retriever breeder how much exercise your particular pup can handle at various ages. Before you get an appropriate answer, the expert must see and feel your Golden pup and must also watch her movement and coordination. This is necessary because every dog grows at her own rate.

Some bone and joint problems are genetic as well, and it's believed these inherited problems can be minimized with proper nutrition and exercise control. Common sense applies. When your roly-poly Golden pup is three or four months old, let her pick her own pace and don't push her into any exercise that might damage forming bones, joints, tendons and ligaments.

Does a senior Golden require much exercise?

Not much. She'll appreciate fetching the morning paper and maybe she'll find her tennis ball later on when she has time. She'll take a dip in the pond and paddle about for a few minutes. Mostly, she just enjoys a nice leisurely walk in a shady park where she can enjoy your company and reminisce about her longer swims in the lake when she was younger.

What can happen if my Golden doesn't get the exercise she needs?

Physical exercise is critical to a Golden's normal development as a puppy, and it continues to be important throughout her life. Muscles will only

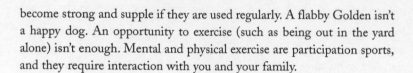

become strong and supple if they are used regularly. A flabby Golden isn't a happy dog. An opportunity to exercise (such as being out in the yard alone) isn't enough. Mental and physical exercise are participation sports, and they require interaction with you and your family.

What can I do if my schedule doesn't permit me the time to exercise my Golden?

Dogs who don't get enough physical and mental activity suffer greatly from boredom. And that can lead to behavior problems, destructiveness, excessive barking, compulsive behaviors and even self-mutilation. Too many Goldens wind up in rescue organizations or shelters because their owners' schedules didn't leave their dogs enough exercise and interaction time. If your schedule is so tight that it doesn't have room for compromise, and you honestly don't have enough time to spend with your companion, don't get a Golden.

What if my schedule isn't consistent?

If your spare time comes at irregular hours, don't worry. It may require more planning on your part, but be as regular and consistent as possible week by week, because dogs have a tough time adjusting to inconsistency. Use your time intelligently when it's available. Don't overdo one type of exercise and skip another, and do the best you can. Your Golden will work with your irregular hours and accept your efforts.

What if I live in an apartment?

Maybe you need the services of a professional dog walker or a teenage neighbor if your work or commuting time takes all your daylight hours. Some large cities have doggy day-care centers that provide supervised areas in which dogs can run and play with each other. Be sure you're comfortable with the management and references of such businesses. If you are really dedicated to your Golden, you can probably give her sufficient quality time and exercise in the early mornings, evenings and weekends.

What if I have an active social life?

You'll be surprised to learn that many dog lovers share their time with their canine companions *and* their human friends. That's easy if you can balance your social life between human-only activities and those that include your Golden pal. If it's not an option for you, you must make a choice: either change social circles or don't get a Golden Retriever.

Can I let my dog run free during the day?

No! Not ever! Keep her behind a fence any time she's not on a leash. Don't let your Golden out of your sight, even in a dog park, and don't leave her under the supervision of strangers. Running free can be extremely costly. No matter how well trained she is or how slow traffic is, any place that's near a street or roadway is no place for a Golden to play.

What if I don't have a fenced-in yard?

- **Can I tie my Golden out?** In a word, no! Few dogs do well when tied up most of the time. Historically, Mastiff-type dogs were tied up during the day and loosed at night to patrol and guard estates. That doesn't exactly describe the Golden's role in her home in modern times. A dog alone in a yard mostly sleeps and is bored all day, and a dog tied up alone in a yard has the added frustration and discomfort of being tied—and the added danger of hurting herself by getting tangled in the rope. If you don't have a fenced-in yard, keep your dog inside.

- **How about a running line?** A running line is a tightly stretched, heavy wire, secured at either end to a pole or tree at a height that is just above a tall man's head. When you snap the dog's leash to the wire, it allows the dog to move freely between the trees. If the distance is 30 or 40 feet and there's no impediment in the path, such as bushes, flowers, posts and so forth, the Golden can certainly run for that distance and get some exercise. But it's simply another method of tying out your Golden, and you shouldn't use it except for very brief periods when you can monitor her.

  Running lines often run into snags. For instance, if the dog circles the tree at one end, she's apt to remain stuck there until someone rescues her. You must provide a shelter to protect the dog from the sun and rain, but the shelter also provides something to wrap the leash around. You can fasten food and water bowls to the ground, but they may be jerked from their moorings, turned over by the leash or tangled in it. Often, when the owner returns home, the Golden has her leash securely wrapped around a tree, and the path under the running line is strewn with a dog bed, an upside-down doghouse, and overturned food and water dishes. It's not the best way to provide exercise for a dog. And remember, an exercise area only gives the Golden an *opportunity* to run; it doesn't supply her with any *reason* to do so.

- **Will an invisible fence work?** An invisible fence is actually a wire that's buried under a few inches of soil around the boundaries of your property. The wire is connected to a transmitter that sends a signal through the wire that's received by a special collar, which delivers a mild electric shock to your dog. When your Golden approaches the perimeter of your property, she receives a shock that becomes greater as she moves nearer to the buried boundary wire. When the fence works the way it is supposed to, your Golden trots toward the unseen boundary, receives a deterring jolt, turns, and walks or runs the other way. Once she has worked out the boundary area, she will stay back from the invisible line most of the time.

  However, an invisible fence doesn't stop other animals from coming in. That means other dogs can come and pick a fight with your Golden. Cats and squirrels can casually meander onto your property, and when the Golden is running hard toward the boundary in hot pursuit, she may charge across despite the shock. Now she's outside the boundary and won't return home regardless of how much she wants to, because the shock collar won't allow her to cross the barrier to go back home.

  An invisible fence also does not protect your dog from people who steal dogs (this happens more often than you might think) or from people who tease or torment dogs. If this happens, your dog has no means to run away, and therefore may be more likely to bite to protect herself.

  Your Golden could also lose the collar, and is then free to come and go as she wants to. Used alone, without any other form of containment, it's dangerous at best. Please don't bet your Golden's life on an invisible fence.

What's the best backyard exercise for a dog?

A fenced yard only furnishes the *opportunity* for exercise. Golden exercise usually includes your participation at least once or twice every day. When you're home, play catch or fetch with her, teach her to catch a Frisbee or build some agility obstacles and teach her to compete. In between these exercise times, give her a yard ball to bump and chase around or a large feeding cube filled with kibble. And when you're home, keep her in the house with you. That's where she wants to be.

How can I exercise my Golden without a fenced yard?

Newly acquired puppies are easily exercised by supervised play and walking on a leash several times a day. Be careful to not allow your pup to meet stray dogs or wild animals on these walks until she has had her vaccinations. Play games in the house, as well. These house games are always fun and can be as energy-consuming as you desire.

Spend your spare weekend time with your companion and take her hiking or camping, but until she's a year old, you should limit her total time on the trail. After she's full grown, she'll be able to carry a pack with enough of her food in it for an overnight trip and a water bottle as well. Beware of packs in warm, humid climates, though, because they can initiate skin problems—which Goldens are so prone to.

Buy a long, retractable leash that will allow her more freedom than a standard leash. Drive her to the beach, a nearby park, the woods or into the country. Pack a picnic lunch for yourself and a snack for her. Take her to areas where she can exercise at her own pace on a surface other than asphalt or concrete. If the park has a lake that allows dogs, let her swim for half an hour. Toss her ball or a retrieving dummy into the water and watch her retrieve it. You'll find she will develop wonderful habits when you're on walks, and you'll reap more benefits than you ever imagined. The long walk won't hurt your health either, and both you and your Golden will be tired out by suppertime.

Can I exercise my Golden beside my bicycle?

At first that sounds like a good way to get some exercise for yourself and give your Golden some roadwork, but it's not really a good idea. Think about it: You're pedaling along with your Golden running beside you when a cat darts out from nowhere and runs across the street in front of you. The next instant you're lying tangled in a mess of twisted bike spokes and your Golden is standing on top of you whining because you wouldn't let her play with the kitty. Or perhaps she is licking your wounds—or her own. If this takes place in traffic, the results could be disastrous.

What about rollerblading with my Golden?

Some American towns have paved dozens of miles of wide trails for biking, roller skating, running and walking. If those trails are available and if it's legal to take your dog on the trail, try it out. Rollerblading usually means you'll be moving rapidly, so be sure she's mature enough for the strenuous exercise involved. Don't forget that you're traveling on wheels and she's not. Keep your speed down, because you and she can become tangled in her leash if either of you lose your footing.

Can my puppy jog with me?

If your pup has finished her puppyhood vaccinations, is past three months of age, and especially if the jogging trail is sod or packed beach sand, a limited amount of jogging is fine. As she matures, you can increase the distance, and by the time she's a year old, she'll be ready for any distance you are. Remember that your dog always has her fur coat on and needs more water than you do while she's exercising. Pad burns may result from running on pavement, so she should be started on very short distances so her pads can toughen up gradually.

How do I exercise my Golden's mind?

Mental exercise is as vital to a Golden's development as physical exercise. Goldens are occasionally accused of being a tad lazy physically, but they are creative rascals. They love to show off their brainpower, and if you want to develop it to the maximum degree, you should give your dog problems to solve. Play hide-and-seek, give her scent training, even if you don't intend to compete in tracking trials. Let her use her natural talents and capabilities, and encourage her to hone her powers of reasoning.

What happens if my Golden doesn't get enough mental stimulation?

She'll get bored and become a nuisance. A bored Golden is a dog in trouble, especially during the first two or three years. A young, inquisitive and bored Golden is like a teenager with too much time on her hands and nothing to do. She'll begin looking for ways to get attention, whether or not they're appropriate. She may wear you out playing games she knows over and over, because that's what you've taught her to do. She may use her intelligence to escape from the backyard or dash out the front door when you least expect it. If you suppress her mental expression by lock and key, she'll become melancholy. In other words, a Golden without mental stimulation is a dull, miserable dog.

What if I want to get involved in tracking trials?

Begin by attending a tracking demonstration without your pet and talking to the competitors. Then join their club and begin formal training. When you see her working and following her first trail, you'll be amazed. Your appreciation of your companion's ability will double and triple with each new accomplishment.

What about hunting with my dog?

If you're a weekend sports person and enjoy hunting game fowl, your Golden's retrieving instincts will serve you well with very little advanced training. She should undoubtedly receive some early gun training, and if you continue to work with her using feathered dummies and waterfowl scents, she should perform well for you. When she's routinely fetching the dummies from water, try her in the company of an already trained water retriever. You'll be surprised how quickly she responds.

What are retriever tests and trials?

This rapidly growing sport is flourishing and fun. Your Golden Retriever was born with a nose for the hunt, and chances are she can prove it at a field event, either a hunt test or a field trial.

Dogs at hunting tests and trials are judged on their natural scenting ability, their swiftness in the field, their style, determination and marking aptitude (*marking* means remembering where a shot bird fell). They must retrieve birds from both land and water, with different testing levels requiring them to mark increasingly difficult falls and multiple birds, and find other birds guided solely by their handler's directions (called a *blind retrieve*).

What's the difference between a hunt test and a field trial? In general, a *hunt test* is not really competitive. Instead, the dogs must perform up to a certain standard in order to pass. But at a *field trial* the dogs compete against one another to earn placements and points. The American Kennel Club and United Kennel Club sanction hunting tests and trials at which dogs can earn titles, as do several other organizations, including the North American Hunting Retriever Organization and the North American Versatile Hunting Dog Association.

How do I get started in hunting tests and trials?

Local gun shops, hunting clubs and gun clubs will likely have information about upcoming hunting events. You can also consult your local Golden Retriever club secretary for a schedule. Plan to attend a trial. Ask the advice of other participants, and try to make some contacts with people who may help as training partners.

What other canine sports can my Golden and I participate in?

If competition is more to your liking, many types of canine competition will give you both plenty of exercise and increase your Golden's focus and trainability. Agility is a canine obstacle course. Flyball is a relay race that includes catching a tennis ball, and a Frisbee competition is an extension of one of the Golden's favorite retrieving games. Obedience isn't an endeavor that yields an abundance of physical exercise, but it involves plenty of mental stimulation. Freestyle competitions are new to the canine world, but they're just the ticket for dogs and masters who enjoy dancing together to music. Canine Good Citizen certification is another excellent avenue to take if you want something less exacting than obedience training, but want to develop your Golden into a better, more obedient pet.

- **What are obedience trials?** In *obedience trials,* dog and handler must perform a variety of exercises, from a simple sit to a complex heel in a figure-8 pattern, demonstrating supreme control and attentiveness throughout. Conformation, coat quality or colors aren't important in this event. The important thing is how she focuses on your directions and how happy it makes her when she pleases you. If your Golden constantly watches you, looking for your signals, she will be very competitive and will love the training.

  Training for an AKC obedience trial is useful in many ways, and your Golden will use and appreciate most of the obedience lessons learned for the rest of her life. And certainly, pursuing advanced titles in obedience work is well within the scope of your Golden.

- **What are agility trials?** An *agility trial* is another career open to a Golden. It's a timed event in which a competing dog races from obstacle to obstacle. A competitor must run through or over those obstacles in a particular sequence as her handler runs alongside, signaling to indicate which obstacle is next. The course is run off-leash, and it demonstrates the ultimate control to have your Golden perform well in spite of barking dogs and screaming onlookers. Many Golden owners believe those trials are the ultimate experience for trainable Golden Retrievers, who have a terrific sense of humor and love to play.

  Begin training your dog when he is young (keeping jump training low, for reasons we discussed earlier), and enter formal agility trials after your companion is a year old. You can build the obstacles and practice at home if you have a big backyard, or you might locate a club to join and use their equipment. If you're planning to build the obstacles, you'll need to contact the AKC for a full description and the exact sizes and dimensions of each obstacle.

  Watching an agility trial is a joy for the audience, but participating and winning the various titles awarded in every stage of training must be the ultimate achievement for an active Golden Retriever.

- **What is canine freestyle?** *Freestyle* is also known as doggie dancing, musical freestyle or heel work to music. It had its origin in obedience trials, and more specifically in heeling off lead. In heeling off lead, the dog must focus on his handler constantly, anticipating every move and deciding instantly on his response. Freestyle today is a choreographed routine performed to musical accompaniment. It involves some costuming, some obedience training, some rhythm and lots of coordination. It combines the expertise of canine obedience with the glamour of equine dressage. It's dog training at its peak, and competitions can be beautiful to watch.

In a typical routine, the dog performs turns, direction changes and other movements that are timed to his handler's actions and a few whispered commands. Dogs whirl around, duck under the handler's legs, move behind the handler, lead or follow her. Appropriate recorded music accompanies the routine, and the handler cues the routine to the music. A handler must have some dancing talent as well as loads of patience to make the routine work, but when well-practiced and performed, the total effect is surprisingly smooth and beautiful.

- **What about Frisbee competitions?** If you think that Frisbee is just a game you play in the park with your Golden, think again. Today, nearly every state has a canine Frisbee organization, and the sport isn't limited to purebred dogs.

  Frisbee dog and disc dog competitions will test your Golden's agility, leaping ability and precision timing. Like other contests, his expertise will depend on training and practice, but the sport is ready-made for a versatile Golden.

  In formal Frisbee contests, your dog may compete in *freeflight* competition, in which the handler throws discs from any location and doesn't wait for the dog to retrieve them. The judges count the number of catches made in 90 seconds and award points from 1 to 10 for showmanship, execution and leaping ability. You can train your Golden to jump over your back to make a catch, or she may catch two discs at once. She may also pivot and twist and make other fanciful movements as she plays to her audience.

  In the *throw and catch* competition, a thrower's circle is laid out and the handler tosses a Frisbee from within the circle. The dog catches and retrieves it as many times as possible in 90 seconds.

- **What is flyball?** *Flyball* is a relay race in which dogs compete in teams of four. During a run, each dog must jump over hurdles to reach a spring-loaded box that contains a tennis ball. When the dog steps on the box's pedal, the ball leaps from the box. The dog catches the ball and returns back over the hurdles. Then the next dog on the team goes. It's a sport that attracts Golden owners who are looking for another outlet for their dogs' energy.

9

Where Should I Get My Golden Retriever?

 Am I truly ready for a new puppy? • Should I buy my spouse a surprise puppy? • What is the best time of year to get a Golden? • Do I want a male or female? • Would I be happier with an older dog? • Is it easy to obtain a Golden Retriever? • What is a responsible breeder? • How do I find such a breeder? • What can I expect the breeder to ask me? • What do I need to ask the breeder? • What is a show-quality puppy? • What is a pet-quality puppy? • What is meant by form and function? • How soon can I take home my puppy? • What about the Internet or a pet shop? • Where do the puppies in pet shops come from? • Can I trust newspaper ads to find a good Golden pup? • I feel sorry for this sick puppy. Can I take him home and nurse him back to health? • What is Golden Retriever rescue? • Can a rescued Golden make a good pet?

Am I truly ready for a new puppy?

It doesn't hurt to ask yourself that question one more time before you take the plunge. Acquiring a new Golden puppy is a challenging experience. It's not all cuddling and wrestling. It's not child's play. It is serious part-time employment for a mature and dedicated person. Golden ownership is an enjoyable endeavor that's always gratifying but isn't always amusing. It requires long walks in inclement weather, grooming and taking care of a dog in sickness and in health. It's sharing a commitment, reciprocal loyalty and dedication with another living being for the next 10 to 12 years.

How much and what kind of space does a puppy require?

A spacious, fenced backyard is ideal but not really necessary. A large home with an extra room for the pup's bed and toys is the ultimate, but unnecessary as well. Tiled, easily cleanable floors are perfect, but sometimes not available. Ideal situations are rarely found, yet thousands of Goldens find their way into loving homes annually. If you can give sufficient time to your new companion, the actual space he occupies can easily be shared with his human family.

Do I have the patience to take on this responsibility?

A quick temper can ruin the relationship you're seeking. If you have a tendency to yell at the kids, don't let that spill over onto your Golden companion. You should be flexible so you can love and correct him at the same time. You must tolerate his character flaws while waiting for lessons to soak in, and you should never expect immediate and total understanding. You must recognize the faults in your dog that you can correct and accept those that are uncorrectable.

Am I financially ready for another obligation?

The financial responsibility of dog ownership is no problem in many American families. However, the additional expense may prevent you from spending money on something else. Remember that buying in haste will enable you to repent at leisure. Pet ownership is an ongoing financial burden that should be carefully calculated before you think about acquiring a Golden.

What's my commitment?

For true dog lovers, canine commitment probably ranks close on the heels of other serious life decisions such as choosing a mate, selecting a career, forming a business and buying a home. Your dog will be with you a minimum of 10 to 12 years, and you must accept that commitment before you acquire any dog at any time. If you aren't committed to the total care of your Golden for the long haul, or if this plan risks floundering or being forgotten in a few months, don't proceed.

Whose advice should I seek to be sure?

This important decision should include advice from several people, including your soul mate or spouse, your family, your veterinarian, dog-loving friends and friends who hate dogs. The more opinions you hear, the better equipped you'll be to make an honest decision. Some people simply aren't suited to dog ownership, and if that includes you, please don't get a Golden Retriever.

Should I buy my spouse a surprise puppy?

If you're considering a Golden as a gift for anyone, please rethink that idea. A lifelong companion shouldn't be presented like a ceramic knick-knack. Acquiring a Golden requires planning and the total agreement of all concerned. There is also a very personal quality about choosing a dog, and each person or family must make that choice for themselves.

What is the best time of year to get a Golden?

The winter holiday season (or any holiday time) is a poor time to get a dog, because he'll arrive when the house is in upheaval, and that can set his adjustment back by weeks. The best time isn't necessarily when the flowers are blooming or the grass is green, either. If your business obligations are lowest in the spring, that's the best time, but if your slack time is in the fall, that's the best time. Weather can be a factor, as can the school year, vacations and long-standing obligations. Your marriage, divorce, baby arrival, moving possibilities and other events can also be factors to consider. Choose a time when everyone has loads of spare time to devote to this important project so they can give the Golden their undivided attention.

Do I want a male or female?

Mostly, gender is a matter of personal preference. Golden breeders and owners have different views on this subject, and you should consult with the breeder you get your dog from. Perhaps females are a bit more dominant, but often males are more submissive and thus are very easily trained. If your companion will be neutered, the sex is immaterial. Neither sex has puppy attributes that overshadow the other, and all pups have the same needs and problems.

Would I be happier with an older dog?

If you aren't sure you can tolerate the bad habits and clumsiness of a puppy, you should think about starting with an adult Golden. He might be one from a responsible breeder—a dog who was kept to show or compete in field trials but didn't quite make the cut, or one who has now retired from competition. Or he might be a rescued dog who desperately needs a home. The many benefits of having an older dog often outweigh the fun of having a roly-poly puppy underfoot. Patience is still necessary with an older dog, but some of the hard puppy-raising work has already been done.

Is it easy to obtain a Golden Retriever?

If you're serious about wanting a Golden Retriever, you'll find one—either a puppy or one who has been in another home. Nearly every state is blessed with a number of responsible Golden breeders, and many breed clubs and Golden Retriever rescue organizations are listed in the last section of this book. No matter how great this breed is or what the demand may be, there are always a few Goldens seeking new homes.

What is a responsible breeder?

One who is devoted to Golden Retrievers. A responsible breeder never breeds a dog unless she believes the resulting litter will make a positive contribution to the breed. She has all her breeding stock examined and cleared for as many genetic flaws as possible. She's a person who understands and loves the breed and isn't particularly interested in making a huge profit.

She won't part with her puppies for minimal prices, either. She places each puppy in a responsible and knowledgeable home with owners who will nurture and train the pup, because she knows a well-mannered Golden is a happy Golden. She understands the form and function of each Golden. She is willing to answer your questions for the life of her dogs, and is also willing to take them back at any time. The conscientious breeder of quality Goldens is serious about her business. She breeds for many desirable qualities, including temperament. She shares her spare time with her dogs. Breeding is intertwined with showing or exhibiting her dogs. The serious breeder thrives on and invites competition and is naturally proud when her dog is judged to be the best.

Most reputable breeders are active in an all-breed club, a Golden Retriever club, one or two competitive sports and perhaps at least one rescue organization. They also insist that owners spay or neuter their pet puppies.

How do I find such a breeder?

You may need to dig deeply to find just the right breeder, because you can't find them around every corner. You can search the Internet for breeders, keeping in mind that the Internet doesn't differentiate between *breeders* and *responsible breeders*. Contact the Golden Retriever Club of America for a referral, or a local Golden Retriever club (you'll find contact information in the last section of this book). Often, local veterinarians will have an idea of who the best breeders are in your area.

Usually you can tell a reputable breeder by the questions she asks. If she's serious about her dogs and is looking for great homes for her pups, she's probably not just one of the crowd of Golden producers who are out for a quick buck. That means she'll put you through the ringer before she'll let you take home one of her pups.

What can I expect the breeder to ask me?

A reputable breeder will ask you about your family circumstances, including how many rooms are in your home and if you've ever owned a Golden or any other dog. She'll quiz you about your temperament, your spare time and whether or not you're a light sleeper. She'll want to know what your facilities are and where your Golden will be housed.

Here are some questions the breeder may ask you:

- Who will be the principal caregiver and trainer for the Golden?
- How much time will you devote to your Golden?
- How big is your home? In what type of region is it located (urban, suburban or rural)?
- Do you have children? How many? What ages?
- Do you have a swimming pool? Is it fenced puppy tight?
- Is your backyard securely fenced? How big is it? Is it shady?
- Where will the Golden sleep?
- Do you and your family travel a lot?
- Are you and your family active, outdoorsy people?
- What are your plans for training your Golden?
- Are you interested in canine sports? What type?
- Is anyone in your family allergic to dogs?
- Do you have time to groom your dog regularly?
- Are you sensitive about dog hair around the house?
- Do you work away from home? How many hours each day?
- Who will care for your dog when you're away on vacation?
- Are you able to leave work during the day to check on the puppy? Can you arrange for someone else to do it?
- Have you ever owned a large dog?
- What happened to your last dog?
- Why are you interested in a Golden?
- Have you had any experience with Goldens?
- Have you discussed the purchase with your spouse and children?
- Will you use a crate as part of your training?

- Do you intend to show the dog? What is your showing experience?
- Do you intend to breed your puppy when it's an adult? Why or why not?
- Will you sign a document that guarantees that you will have your dog spayed or neutered before six months of age?
- Can you afford a Golden and his vaccinations, food, equipment and health care?
- Will you sign a document giving me first right of refusal to take your pup back if you can't keep him?

What do I need to ask the breeder?

The critical thing to cover is her knowledge and experience with the Golden breed, and this should take you about half an hour. Ask for a tour of her kennel, but if she's an average Golden breeder, she'll probably say you're in it. That's because most reputable Golden fanciers raise their litters in their home.

Here are some questions to ask a reputable Golden breeder, followed by some advice about what answers to look for.

- Who is your veterinarian, and may I call the animal hospital for a personal reference? (A responsible breeder will have a close relationship with a veterinarian, and will be happy to tell you who it is.)
- Do you own both the sire and dam, and if not, where is the sire? If the sire isn't present, have you a picture of him and a copy of his pedigree? (Just make sure the sire isn't the neighbor's dog, a cousin's dog or a dog down the street. Both dam and sire should be carefully selected for each breeding.)
- Is the sire a winning show dog, retriever trialer, obedience dog or gundog? Has the dam earned conformation championship points or retriever trial or obedience placements, or is she a good gundog? (These are indications of the quality of the dogs involved in the breeding.)
- May I see and handle the dam? (Puppies often take after their mother. She should be fit and healthy, friendly and happy.)
- Are the dam's and sire's hips and elbows OFA certified? May I see copies of their certificates? (See Chapter 10 for more on what this means.)

- Have both parents been examined for PRA, certified by CERF and cleared for as many congenital problems that afflict Goldens as possible? May I see copies of those certificates? (See Chapter 10 for more on what this means.)

- Has a veterinarian examined the pups' hearts? What veterinarian, and when did he do this? (Goldens can be susceptible to some hereditary heart problems, especially subvalvular aortic stenosis—SAS. Make sure the pups have been examined.)

- Do intractable skin problems occur in your bloodline? (Skin problems are very common in Goldens, and most lines have some individuals with mild skin problems. But dogs with serious skin problems should never be bred.)

- Are you aware of hypothyroidism in your bloodline? (Dogs with hypothyroidism should never be bred.)

- How long have you raised Goldens? (The longer, the better.)

- How many litters do you average each year? (It should be no more than one or two.)

- Do you have any pictures of prior litters from the same parents? (A good breeder will have piles and piles of pictures of her puppies, and they will all look fat and healthy.)

- Do you keep track of your puppies after they're sold? (The answer should be yes.)

- Are you active in the local or state Golden Retriever breed, obedience, agility or field trial club? (A good breeder is active with her dogs, constantly proving their worth through competition.)

- Are most of your pups sold to hunters, pet families, show families, agility or obedience competitors? (This matters if you are looking for a dog to enter in competitions.)

- What percentage of pet puppies do you expect from this litter? (The majority of puppies in any litter will be pets, but the breeder should also expect some standouts for the show ring or for a canine sport. If she doesn't, there was no reason to breed the litter.)

- What's the price of a nice pet puppy? A show prospect? (A show prospect should cost quite a bit more. See Chapter 10 for more on what a Golden Retriever costs.)

- At what age do you allow your pups to go to new homes? (It should never be less than eight weeks.)
- Have the puppies been vaccinated? When, and by whom? Do you have certificates? (The puppies should have one set of vaccinations before they go to their new homes.)
- Have the puppies been checked for worms? (The answer should be yes.)
- When do you begin handling the pups? How has the litter been socialized? (The pups should be handled from birth, and should be raised underfoot with as many different kinds of people and experiences as possible.)
- Will you take the pup back if I can't keep him for any reason? (The answer should be yes.)
- Do you routinely do personality testing? (The answer should be yes.)

What is a show-quality puppy?

Golden breeders often raise one or two litters each year from one or two prize bitches. The breeder might select *one* puppy as a show-quality puppy from one of those carefully calculated matings. Usually the breeder keeps that nearly perfect puppy for several months, or perhaps until she shows him in puppy matches. If he's a show prospect, he might go on to finish his championship and she may choose him to become one of the breeding stock. Such a pup is a rare find, and will obviously cost more money than a pet. Breeders may also be very reluctant to sell a show-quality puppy to a novice Golden owner.

What is a pet-quality puppy?

The breeder might evaluate the remainder of pups from each litter and find one or two with gundog characteristics that indicate field trial prospects. After she chooses these special show-quality and gundog puppies, she usually sells the remaining Golden puppies as pets. These pet or companion puppies are genetically as good as the prized show puppies, but they often have very tiny flaws that separate them from show-quality pups and designate them as pet-quality puppies. They will make great companions.

What is meant by form and function?

A laid-back Golden might be a fine companion, but isn't necessarily a good choice for a competition dog. If you want a performance Golden, check with the breeder. If she speaks of a correct *form* to fit a particular *function*, she's probably giving you the straight scoop. If a dog has perfect conformation for field trials, he's not necessarily the right choice for the show ring. Another Golden's physical structure might predispose him to fatigue in the field, but he could be a classic show dog.

How soon can I take home my puppy?

You can always make quick cash-and-carry purchases when you're dealing with a questionable breeder. Most reputable breeders raise only a couple of litters a year, with only one or two outstanding pups in each, so if you wanted a show pup, you might be far down the list and your wait might be more than a year. If you're seeking a pet puppy, you probably won't have to wait terribly long. And if you're the first qualified buyer to choose from an eight-week-old litter, you could take your pup home the same day or within a few days.

I just want a nice pet and I don't have the time to find a *responsible breeder*. What about the Internet or a pet shop?

Golden Retriever clubs are listed on the Internet by states, and that's not a bad way to search for a reputable breeder. If you like Internet shopping, first go to the AKC's home page. Then, under Golden Retriever, contact the secretary of your state's Golden club. Ask for names of breeders in your area, and if they have web pages, contact them.

Even when you buy a puppy from someone who is a member of a club, though, the risks are significant. Shopping for a puppy on the Internet means you're buying *sight unseen,* because you can't handle the puppy or his parents or talk to the breeder one on one or see the facilities in which he was raised. You'll get pictures, of course, and maybe even a video, but what you think you see might be slightly misrepresented. People do Internet shopping more and more frequently because of the ease of purchase, but in the final stage of puppy selection, you should always see and handle your puppy and have a personal conversation with the breeder before putting any money down or making a purchase decision.

Pet shops are similar to Internet shopping. In a pet shop, you'll find purebred, registered puppies, but you have no other information with which to make your selection. Usually, the parents' personalities, OFA certifications and CERF examination results aren't available. You can get a pedigree from the AKC when you send for your registration certificate, but unfortunately, that might be too late to chase down all the facts. You don't know if your puppy's sire or dam was a winner in the show ring or field. You can't compare a pup to his siblings or his parents. You're taking a calculated risk on the temperament, personality and conformation of the pup. All Golden puppies are cute and cuddly when they're freshly weaned, and that fact alone keeps many pet shops in business. But while cute sells puppies, it also covers a multitude of possible genetic and developmental faults.

Where do the puppies in pet shops come from?

Generally, they come from puppy farms, also known as puppy mills. Many puppies from large-scale Internet sellers also come from puppy farms. They are usually located on the outskirts of cities, where they're handy to customers. Often they're located in unincorporated regions where zoning laws are lax, so they can easily expand their kennel operations. That's where they might be located, but if you devote your life to looking, you'll be extremely lucky if you can locate a *good* puppy farm anywhere.

Puppy farm owners find a ready source of breeding stock from amateur backyard breeders who have not devoted any time to studying the breed. They buy cheap Golden females from newspaper ads, or they adopt unspayed pets who must find new homes, paying little or no cash for them. They juggle registration numbers and keep their investment low because their only motive is puppy production and cash in the pocket. They breed bitches each time they come into heat to males who are of equally poor quality. They produce as many puppies as possible every year and sell them for many times more than they're worth. Some of these puppies are grossly inbred, others are outcrosses (breeding two totally unrelated individuals of the same breed). A pedigree from such a farm isn't worth the paper it's printed on because records are related to income, not puppy quality.

Puppy farms can be differentiated from reputable breeders by many factors, a few of which are listed below.

- Many pups are available from several different breeds.
- Rarely is there any evidence of participation in any canine sports, such as conformation shows, obedience, field trials, agility, etc.
- You'll see no pictures of favorite Goldens from the past.
- Breeding dams usually are in a questionable nutritional state, and their puppies are often potbellied and less active than expected.
- Litters are kept in questionable or downright dirty environments.
- You'll see evidence of poor diets and cheap, bulk dog food.
- Puppies haven't been socialized and often are shy.
- Very young puppies of different breeds all kept together in outdoor, dirt runs.
- The area is often stinky, rank and poorly kept.
- Few if any pedigrees of pups are available, but if you want to pay for one, it will be furnished.
- The owner is interested only in your money, and couldn't be less interested in your expectations or the kind of home you will provide for the pup.

Isn't it possible to get a good dog from a puppy farm or a pet shop?

It is possible, but it pretty much depends on chance. Do you really want to trust such an important choice to nothing but luck?

If you're seeking a *cheap* puppy, that's a different story. Cheap, that is, if you consider only the initial cost. Many times those vendors sell AKC-registered pups at a much lower price than you'd expect to pay, especially after you've talked to reputable breeders or friends who have recently bought a nice Golden. You might not pick up on what a puppy farm owner's motives are, because it appears that the farm has everything you're seeking. Their Golden puppies are AKC-registered, so they must be OK, right? Not by a long shot! The AKC is a dog registry, not a regulatory agency. The AKC has rules that are designed to make sure purebred dogs are really pure (and even these rules can be bent by unscrupulous breeders who walk a fine line, just inside the limits), but AKC registration is no guarantee of a dog's health or quality.

Can I trust newspaper ads to find a good Golden pup?

People who advertise in the pet advertisement section of a newspaper may be totally trustworthy, reputable breeders, or they may be backyard breeders or puppy farm owners. The ads naturally won't tell you which type they are, so you must call them and then go visit the advertised litter.

What is a backyard breeder?

A backyard breeder is someone who probably cares deeply about their dogs, but hasn't done the work to learn about the breed and carefully screen their dogs for genetic and temperament problems. This person is a dabbler who owns a registered Golden female and decides to breed her to the neighbor's registered male. These neophytes often propagate unsuspected hereditary problems quite innocently and without malice. They're looking to their wallets and simply don't know how to do what they're doing.

If I decide to buy a backyard-bred pup, what should I look for?

Read about the breed before you go to see the puppy, and ask the seller everything she knows about the litter. Look carefully at the dam and identify, if you can, any visible faults and flaws. Compare what you see to the breed standard (which you can find on the AKC web site). Below are some clues to ill health and congenital faults:

- Is the puppy lethargic, droopy-eyed or disinterested? A typical Golden puppy is rambunctious, full of fire and ready to go. If the pup you're considering is less that that, beware!

- Are his feet pointing straight forward (as they should be), or do his toes turn outward or inward? Both extremes are very undesirable.

- Are his toes grouped tightly together or are they separated? Splay feet are undesirable, but they may tighten up as he matures. Splay feet are usually accompanied by upward curvature of his metacarpus (wrist) that makes him appear to be walking on his heels. Those signs can be associated with poor nutrition and might not be permanent.

- Does he paddle when he walks? His forefeet should track straight, not in an outward arc.

- Are his hocks (the joint on the back legs that points backward) turned inward and his hind toes pointed outward? This means the pup has poor hind leg angulation and is very undesirable.

- Does he have a fat belly, but his ribs and backbone are showing? A pot-bellied pup is a poorly nourished pup. The problem may be a worm infestation, which is curable. It may be caused by feeding a horrible diet, which (hopefully) also is correctable. It may be caused by an internal defect, such as a hereditary heart disease that probably isn't correctable.

- Does he have diarrhea, as evidenced by fecal stains on his hocks? That may be caused by feeding milk or other improper foods, or it may be a sign of a digestive disorder that could be corrected with diet improvement and medication, or it might be more serious.

- Is there a marble-sized lump in the navel region of his abdomen? That might be an umbilical hernia, which can be fixed surgically. You might want to negotiate the price to cover the required operation.

- Are both testicles descended into his scrotum? Monorchidism (single testicle descended) and cryptorchidism (neither testicle descended) are problems that you should discuss with the vendor before you make your purchase. Both conditions can be corrected surgically, but failure to do so can predispose the dog to cancer of the undescended testicle(s) and bring further expense to you.

- Open his mouth and look at his incisors (front teeth). Do they meet like blades of a scissors, with the top teeth touching the lower ones as they slide over? That's a *scissors bite* and is normal. However, if the upper teeth overlap the lower ones with space in between, that's called an *overbite* or *overshot bite*, which is very undesirable. If his lower teeth protrude outside the upper ones, like a Bulldog's bite, that's called an *undershot bite* and is equally bad.

- Are his gums moist and bright pink, and are his eyes bright and shiny? Dull eyes and pallid or pale gums may be signs of illness and may suggest a heavy internal parasite burden, but other diseases can cause them as well.

- Does he have a watery discharge or pus exuding from his eyes? That's a sure sign that something is wrong with his health. His eyes should be clear and free of any discharge. Watering eyes may be a sign of entropion (a turned-in eyelid), which is a fault that can be surgically corrected for a fee. Green or yellow discharge, accompanied by lethargy, are signs associated with many illnesses, and if you spot them, you should leave quickly without a puppy.

- Is his nose-rubber (the skin on the top and front of his muzzle) black, dark brown or pink? Pink nose-rubber is a fault, but that color may not cause him any permanent problem unless it's very pale or unless he's sensitive to sunburn.

- Is his coat silky, limp or curly? A Golden's coat should be double thickness, dense and waterproof. It's often wavy, but should never be curly.

- Does he have a prominent white star on his chest? Such a white marking anywhere on the body is highly undesirable in the breed, but may be found on poor-quality Goldens. It won't be admired by Golden fanciers but shouldn't detract from his value as a pet.

I feel sorry for this sick puppy. Can I take him home and nurse him back to health?

Everyone is entitled to receive a sound, healthy pup for a fair and equitable price. If you're planning to buy a Golden from any source, find one who at least looks healthy and clean. Callous as it sounds, buying a sick pup is the worst mistake you can make, because in doing so, you are an enabler for the proprietor. Your dollars supply him with the means to continue an unscrupulous and corrupt practice, and you're saddling yourself with years of expense and heartache.

What is Golden Retriever rescue?

Most rescue organizations are staffed by dedicated volunteers who are Golden fanciers. They locate Golden Retrievers who have been given up to shelters, abandoned on streets and virtually any Golden who needs a home. Typically, the rescue group moves the unfortunate dog into a foster home or a well-staffed shelter until they can find another home for the dog. They provide veterinary examinations for the rescued dog and bring him up to date on vaccinations and parasite prevention. The shelter or a foster family cares for the Golden's medical, physical and psychological needs while he is waiting for a new family, and thus saves a precious Golden life.

Rescued Goldens are neutered and the rescue organization provides prospective owners with education, counseling and, to some extent, help with training classes. Often rescue organizations will board one of their former charges while his new owners are away. Some rescues have no kennel facilities, but are simply a collection of Golden Retriever owners or breeders who foster Goldens in their homes. They get their driving energy from their dedication to the breed. Although there are nearly 100 Golden Retriever rescue groups across America, more abandoned Goldens exist than rescue groups can care for.

Can a rescued Golden make a good pet?

Many of the dogs available from rescue kennels are fantastic companions who have bonded with past owners, lost them for some reason and are seeking new homes. Dogs, in general, are instinctively quite malleable, and Golden Retrievers are more flexible than most. Generally, dogs thrive on consistency, but companions from this adaptable breed can and do accept changes, as long as their humans treat them fairly and gently and they can make smooth transitions into new families.

A rescued Golden is a blessing to a new family. More than 90 percent of the adult Goldens in rescue are housebroken, and those that aren't can easily be trained. Usually they have extensive canine social skills and even more human socialization. A mature Golden usually is more predictable than a puppy or a young adult. He's less destructive than a puppy and has a longer attention span, which makes training even easier.

Rescue organizations do report an increase in abandoned Goldens whose temperament is fractious, vicious or aggressive. Goldens with those problems are generally not rehomed.

10

How Do I Register My Golden Retriever?

What does it mean when a dog is registered? • What does registration guarantee? • What is the AKC? • What are a dog's *papers* and what do they cost? • What other registries are doing business in the United States? • What is a pedigree? • What is a title? • What about health guarantees? • Is there an average Golden Retriever price? • What contributes to the price of a Golden Retriever puppy?

What does it mean when a dog is registered?

It simply means a canine registry organization has recorded the dog's birth and parentage. A canine registry maintains a stud book (a record of the breeding particulars of all dogs of recognized breeds), keeps pedigrees and lists of every dog of every breed that applies for registration. Registration simply means that your Golden's parents and her birth are registered by that particular registry. Each registered dog has a registration number in addition to her name, and any recognized titles she earns will be added to her record.

What does registration guarantee?

It should guarantee that your dog is who her registration papers say she is, with the parents and ancestors her pedigree says she has, and is a pure-bred Golden Retriever. In other words, registration is confirmation of breed and identity. It does not guarantee the health or quality of any dog.

But the guarantee of any registration is only as good as the integrity of the registry—and the breeders who use it. Unscrupulous dog breeders have been known to falsify a dam's or sire's registration or the registration of a litter. The AKC (and some other registries) periodically inspects breeding operations, especially large-scale ones, for accuracy of record keeping, and sometimes even refuses to register a litter or rescinds the registration of some dogs. But in reality, registration is still basically an honor system. DNA testing is coming into side use, and may eventually make registration an iron-clad guarantee of parentage. But it hasn't happened yet.

What's the worst I can expect from a registered puppy?

You can buy a registered Golden Retriever with every genetic fault in the book. Registered Goldens can have sour dispositions and horrible person-alities. They can have black spots or white spots, be potbellied and lame, but if the appropriate papers have been filed, they're still registered. Registration only means their parents were registered, and it has no connotation of value. Beware of anyone who sells Golden pups whose only virtue is that they are registered. The value of a purebred Golden lies in the hands of a breeder.

What is the AKC?

AKC is an abbreviation for American Kennel Club, the largest canine registry in the United States. The AKC recognizes about 150 breeds, including the Golden Retriever. AKC records the pedigrees of all registered dogs and the names of winning dogs in each authorized event. I have used AKC for reference in this book because it is the best-known canine registry in America.

As the keeper of the breed standards (which are actually written by the national breed clubs), AKC sanctions many canine sporting events and licenses judges for these events. A national breed club for each breed, more commonly known as the *parent club*, develops the breed standard that the AKC adopts.

AKC has many rules, but it is not a regulatory organization; it does not enforce breeding standards or regulate the quality of puppies produced by breeders.

Who is a member of the AKC?

The AKC has no individual members. Instead, it is a club of clubs. The AKC recognizes a single national parent club for each breed. (I have listed the Golden Retriever parent club in the last section of this book.) The parent club is made up of people with extensive experience in the breed. There are also a number of Golden Retriever specialty clubs in the United States. A specialty club is made up of groups of Golden fanciers from a particular region or locality. Sometimes specialty clubs are also AKC-member clubs.

What are a dog's *papers* and what do they cost?

Papers are the puppy's registration certificate, and her papers may also include her pedigree, her vaccination and health certificate and a copy of any contract you might have made with the breeder. Her papers also might include copies of your agreement to have her spayed and at what age that will be done, printed dietary recommendations and the date she'll need to return to a veterinarian for booster vaccinations. Papers should be free from the breeder (although you will ultimately have to pay a fee to the AKC to register your dog).

What if the breeder tells me the papers will be ready later?

Walk away. You have no guarantee the breeder has actually registered the puppy's litter—or ever will. And you have no way to register your dog on your own; the breeder *must* begin the process. The AKC cannot step in to mediate in these matters, so get the papers in your hand along with the dog. The breeder must register the litter by the time a pup is ready to go to her new home.

What's a litter registration?

When a litter is born to registered parents, the breeder must send in official notification to the AKC. The AKC sends back a litter registration, which is a preliminary or temporary registration that lists the pups' sire, dam and their registration numbers. A litter registration has a page for each puppy that lists the puppy's sex, date of birth and color. The litter registration page for your pup should accompany her when you take her home, and you should check to be sure it matches her description. You send it to the AKC together with a chosen name (the breeder may insist upon his kennel name as a prefix), date, your name and the registration fee. If you don't do this, your puppy will not be registered.

What's a limited registration?

A limited registration is a special kind of registration, designated by the breeder, that says the pup can enter events and shows as an AKC-registered dog, but the AKC won't register the pup's offspring. In other words, it's a very useful tool that breeders use to allow dogs to compete, but not reproduce. If the breeder agrees to change it, he may convert this limited registration to a full registration. A puppy sold with limited registration is sometimes a bit less expensive than a fully registered one, because she does not have show and breeding potential.

What other registries are doing business in the United States?

- The United Kennel Club (UKC) is another all-breed registry, and it recognizes more than 300 breeds. For several years, the UKC has embraced DNA testing to prove pedigrees.

- The American Rare Breed Association (ARBA) recognizes and registers about 175 breeds that aren't common in the United States. Those include rare American breeds that have published standards, parent clubs and events, but the two principal all-breed registries don't recognize them.

- In the United States, CKC refers to the Continental Kennel Club, which has an open registry and will maintain pedigrees and registries of crossbred dogs as well as purebreds. It also recognizes more than one standard for each breed.

- The Canadian Kennel Club (CKC) is the Canadian equivalent of the AKC. Many Goldens in the northern states are registered with both the AKC and the CKC.

- Federation Cynologique Internationale (FCI) is an organization based in Thuin, Belgium, that doesn't register dogs but instead maintains breed standards and other records for 80 different countries' national kennel clubs. Its role is to ensure that all members mutually recognize the pedigrees and judges of the 80 FCI-member countries.

There are also various other private registries, some of which register only one breed, and some of which will register any dog whose owner sends in the required fee.

What's the difference between the various registries?

A registry's motives influence its value. If its function is to improve every purebred dog breed that it registers, it should sponsor judged events and competitions. That's a big plus, and is the sign of a dynamic organization. It should have a stated code of ethics and strict rules. The number of ancillary services it has established for member clubs and for the general public is yet another sign of a good registry. The degree to which pedigree information is investigated and the willingness to hear any grievance or petition also set a good registry apart.

Some registries are like the diploma mills that advertise in the back of magazines. Anyone who has the cash and can complete an application can acquire a technical certificate—or register their dog. If you have a dog who looks something like a Golden Retriever, you can probably have her registered by some organization. However, a questionable registration doesn't give her the typical Golden personality, trainability, intelligence or appearance. An honestly registered Golden will be predictable in color, character and temperament, and that's the true value of registration. Anything less is just a piece of paper.

What is a pedigree?

It's a genealogical list of a dog's ancestry—nothing more. Every dog, purebred or mixed breed, has a pedigree. It has no bearing on the quality, value or price of a puppy. A pedigree can be written for any purebred dog or even for a mutt, providing someone knows the names and descriptions of her ancestors. The statement that a pup is pedigreed doesn't necessarily mean she's a purebred. For a modest fee, you can obtain a *certified* pedigree from the AKC that is based on their careful records.

What is a title?

Titles are awards earned by dogs in sanctioned canine competitions. A *Ch.* in front of a Golden's name indicates that she has earned the Champion title in AKC conformation competition. It means several different dog show judges agreed that she was the best of her sex entered in several different shows. The initials following a dog's name represent titles earned in various canine sports, and they mean the dog in question has worked hard and trained hard.

What significance does a title have?

If ancestors who have *Ch.* in front of their names dominate your pup's pedigree, it might be quite significant. However, those titles mean very little if only the most distant relatives have them. The ideal is to see those titles in the most recent generations. In that case, you can be pretty sure that your pup's progenitors measured up in the show ring, on the sporting field, or both.

Remember, you're the most important judge of your dog. If you consider her a champion, that's just what she is! Unless your chief interest is the perfection of her accomplishments, all the titles mentioned above, and more besides, are of little concern. If her personality and companionship are above reproach in your home, and if she pleases you and earns your respect, she's a winner!

What about health guarantees?

There are none, but there are some health problems the breeder can check your Golden's parents for. If the parents are certified clear of these problems, chances are your puppy will be as well. (Of course, parents can be perfectly healthy and still create affected offspring because they may carry a gene for a defect, even they do not have the condition themselves.)

At the very least, you want a Golden whose parents have been tested and certified clear of hip dysplasia, the eye disease PRA, and subaortic stenosis, a heart disease that is common in the breed.

After two years of age, every breeding Golden should be screened for hip dysplasia and elbow dysplasia. These X-rays must be taken in a very precise way, and are sent off to either the Orthopedic Foundation for Animals (OFA) or PennHip, both of which have set up formal procedures for measuring the soundness of a dog's hips and elbows. Both also maintain a registry of the dogs screened, which is an invaluable tool for breeders. The breeder should show you OFA or PennHip certification for your puppy's mother and father.

A veterinary ophthalmologist examines both parents' eyes for signs of progressive retinal atrophy (PRA), a hereditary defect that can lead to blindness. These findings are sent to Canine Eye Registry Foundation (CERF), which reports and records the results for future reference. Ask the breeder to show you proof that the mother and father dog have been registered with CERF. Or you can contact CERF directly to verify that both dogs have been cleared of eye disease.

There is no official organization that tests for subaortic stenosis, but your puppy's breeder should show you something from his veterinarian that certifies both the pup's parents have no heart murmur.

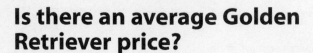

Is there an average Golden Retriever price?

Probably your Golden will cost between $150 and $2,000, depending on her age and her potential. At the bottom of the price range is an adult rescued dog who will be a wonderful pet or companion. At the other extreme is a show-quality puppy destined to be a star in the ring or a top gundog, and eventually to produce more puppies if she performs to expectations. Somewhere in between are pet-quality dogs of various types.

Average is a misleading term to apply to any dog, because it means something different to each person you ask. In any given region, there's an average price for rescue dogs and another for pet-quality puppies and yet another for show or gundog prospects. Let's say an *average* Golden is defined as a typical lovable and loving puppy who grows into a typical trainable adult who is mild-mannered and can be trusted in virtually any situation. She is probably a pet-quality Golden from a fine litter of well-socialized Golden puppies that resulted from a carefully planned mating of two superior parents.

In other words, you'll probably get a wonderful Golden pet if you choose your breeder carefully, as we've already discussed. If you choose a puppy from an amateur backyard breeder, a pet shop or a puppy farm, you'll probably wind up with something less than average, regardless of how the term is defined.

What is a *show* price?

It represents the cost of producing the finest pup out of a fine litter; the best of the best. It's the value of a puppy who has the greatest possible chances for winning in the conformation ring. A show dog is *born*, not developed. Show qualities are the result of a perfect mesh of the genetic backgrounds of many dogs who have been carefully selected. However, dog breeding is still an art, not quite a science, so a great show dog is also the product of great good luck.

What is a *pet* price?

It's the price you pay for a puppy whom a Golden Retriever breeder produced from a fine pair of proven parents. It includes the actual costs borne by that conscientious breeder to achieve perfection in a litter, which, perhaps, may have yielded one puppy that nearly achieved the flawlessness hoped for. The remaining puppies are evaluated and sold as pets or companions to owners like you, who want the best possible pet, but don't intend to show and breed their Golden pup.

What contributes to the price of a Golden Retriever puppy?

The breeder's plan is to mate the best with the best and the best puppies will emerge. The dam and sire were each selected from the somewhat limited pool of top-quality dogs in field or show, and the cost of those two dogs must be considered. Each parent had to be raised, trained, groomed and fed for at least two years before being mated.

Before the nuptials, each of them will be compared to and judged against other fine Goldens in conformation dog shows, obedience trials, field trials and the like. Each of the many shows they enter has a cost attached. Entry fees must be considered, as well as traveling costs, handler fees, hotel charges and, of course, the costs of daily maintenance for dog and handler. When you attend a conformation show or field trial and see the hundreds of beautiful, talented, smart dogs, you must realize that the people are there at their own expense.

A breeding pair will have undergone every screening test possible to rule out genetic diseases and faults, and only then will they be mated and produce a litter. These tests are not cheap. The dam's special nutritional needs, supplements, examinations and possibly professional assistance during delivery, also contribute to the cost of your Golden puppy.

The litter should be raised in a home environment and be well-socialized by the breeder, who also must assist each buyer to select the best puppy to match their particular personality and expectation. He must screen prospective owners and place the puppies in homes well-suited to the pups. Sometimes this takes months instead of weeks, during which time the pups' training, socialization, feeding and care must be provided.

Most breeders only sell puppies who have received a veterinary examination and vaccinations for puppyhood diseases. Those puppies have been checked for worms and other parasites and treated, if necessary. All that having been stated, it's a wonder anyone becomes a purebred dog breeder. Certainly this kind of care and quality has a price.

How Can I Learn More?

Golden Retriever Clubs

Golden Retriever Club of America,
c/o Jolene Carey, Administrative Assistant
P.O. Box 20434, Oklahoma City, OK 73156
www.grca.org/clubs/clubs.htm

This is the national parent club. Contact this club to find a local Golden
Retriever Club in your area or to find a reputable breeder. You can also
find local clubs listed on the AKC web site.

Golden Retriever Rescue

There are too many Golden Retriever rescue groups to list them all here.
The Golden Retriever Club of America should be able to help you find
rescue groups in your area. Also try Yankee Golden Retriever Rescue Inc.,
P.O. Box 808, Hudson, ME, 01749-0808, 978-568-9700, www.ygrr.org

Purebred Dog Clubs

American Kennel Club
5580 Centerview Dr.
Raleigh, NC 27606-3390
919-233-9767
www.akc.org

Field Dog Stud Book
American Field Publishing Co.
542 S. Dearborn St., Suite 1350
Chicago, IL 60605
312-663-9797
www.americanfield.com

United Kennel Club
100 E. Kilgore Rd.
Kalamazoo, MI 49001-5598
616-343-9020
www.ukcdogs.com

Canadian Kennel Club
Commerce Park
89 Skyway Ave., Suite 100
Etobicoke, Ontario, Canada M9W
6R4
416-675-5511
www.canadiankennelclub.com

Hunting Dog Clubs

National Field Retriever
Association
2003 N. Boomer Rd.
Stillwater, OK 74075
www.nfra.us

Hunting Retriever Club
Claudene Christopher, Secretary
P.O. Box 3179
Big Spring, TX 79721-3179
915-267-1659
www.hrc-ukc.com

North American Hunting
Retriever Association
P.O. Box 5159
Fredericksburg, VA 22403
540-286-0625
www.nahra.org

Amateur Field Trial Clubs of
America
360 Winchester Lane
Stanton, TN 38069
www.fielddog.com/aftca/

National Shoot to Retrieve
Association
226 North Mill Street #2
Plainfield, IN 46168
www.nstra.org

North American Versatile
Hunting Dog Association
P.O. Box 529
Arlington Heights, IL 60006
www.navhda.org

Activity Organizations

North American Dog Agility
Council
11522 S. Hwy. 3
Cataldo, ID 83810
208-689-3803
www.nadac.com

North American Flyball
Association
1400 W. Devon Ave., #512
Chicago, IL 60660
800-318-6312
www.flyball.org

United States Dog Agility
Association
P.O. Box 850955
Richardson, TX 75085-0955
972-231-9700
www.usdaa.com

Agility Association of Canada
Rob Chipman, President
957 Seymour Blvd.
North Vancouver, BC
Canada V7J 2J7
604-230-4225
www.aac.ca

Canine Freestyle Federation
21900 Foxden Lane
Leesburg, VA 20175
www.canine-freestyle.org

SkyHoundz
4060-D Peachtree Rd., Suite 326
Atlanta, GA 30319
800-786-9240
www.skyhoundz.com

National 4-H Dog Project Director
National 4-H Council
7100 Connecticut Avenue
Chevy Chase, MD 20815
www.guidestar.org

World Canine Freestyle
  Organization
P.O. Box 350122
Brooklyn, NY 11235-2525
718-332-8336
www.worldcaninefreestyle.org

International Disc Dog Handlers'
  Association
1690 Julius Bridge Road
Ball Ground, GA 30107
770-735-6200
www.iddha.com

Health Organizations

American Animal Hospital
  Association
12575 W. Bayaud Ave.
Lakewood, CO 80228
303-986-2800
www.aahanet.org
www.healthypet.com

American Veterinary Medical
  Association
930 N. Meacham Rd.
Chicago, IL 60173
www.avma.org

Canine Eye Registration Foundation
Veterinary Medical Data Program
South Campus Courts, Building C
Purdue University
West Lafayette, IN 47907
765-494-8179
www.vet.purdue.edu/~yshen/
  cerf.html

National Animal Poison Control
  Center
1717 S. Philo, Suite 36
Urbana, IL 61802
800-548-2423
888-426-4435
www.aspca.org/site/
  PageServer?pagename=apcc

Orthopedic Foundation for Animals
2300 E. Nifong Blvd.
Columbia, MO 65201-3856
573-442-0418
www.offa.org

PennHip
3900 Delancey St.
Philadelphia, PA 19104-6010
www.vet.upenn.edu/research/
  centers/pennhip//

Service Organizations

Delta Society
580 Naches Ave. SW, Suite 101
Renton, WA 98055-2297
425-226-7357
www.deltasociety.org

Therapy Dogs, Inc.
P.O. Box 5868
Cheyenne, WY 82003
877-843-7364
307-432-0272
www.therapydogs.com

Therapy Dogs International
88 Bartley Rd.
Flanders, NJ 07836
973-252-9800
www.tdi-dog.org

Pet Loss Hotlines

University of California, Davis
530-752-4200

Tufts University School of Veterinary Medicine (Massachusetts)
508-839-7966

Virginia-Maryland Regional College of Veterinary Medicine
540-231-8038

Michigan State University College of Veterinary Medicine
517-432-2696

Washington State University College of Veterinary Medicine
509-335-5704

Books

The Complete Dog Book, 19th Edition, Revised, American Kennel Club, Howell Book House, 1998.

The Dog Owner's Home Veterinary Handbook, 3rd Edition, James M. Giffin, M.D., and Liisa D. Carlson, D.V.M., Howell Book House, 2000.

Dog Training in 10 Minutes, Carol Lea Benjamin, Howell Book House, 1997.

Game Dog: The Hunter's Retriever for Upland Birds and Waterfowl: A Concise New Training Method, Richard A. Wolters, E.P. Dutton, 1995.

The Golden Retriever: All That Glitters, Julie Cairns, Howell Book House, 1999.

The Ultimate Golden Retriever, 2nd Edition, Valerie Foss, Howell Book House, 2003.

Index

activities, 113–118, 145–146
activity level, 5–6
adoptions, 9, 11, 13–14, 133–134
aggression, growing problem, 24
agility trials, 117
AKC (American Kennel Club), 9–10, 104, 117, 137–138, 140
allergies, 49–50
American Animal Hospital Association, 9
American Association of Feed Control Officials (AAFCO), 65–66
American Rare Breed Association (ARBA), 139
apartments, 103, 110
associative learning, training, 97–98
Australian Cattle Dog, 10

baths, frequency of, 83
behavior problems, 24, 31–32, 93
biting, mouthing versus, 24
blood, genetic diseases, 47–48
Bloodhound, 4
bones, 47, 77, 109
books, 147
breed description, 2, 4–5
breeders, 11–12, 80, 123–134, 141–143
breeding, pet owner issues, 56–57
breed purpose, 2–4
breed quality, 11–12
brushes, grooming aid, 80

Canadian Kennel Club (CKC), 139
Canine Eye Registry Foundation (CERF), 141
canine freestyle, 117–118
Canine Good Citizen (CGC), 104
canned foods, 71–72
Champion (Ch.) title, 140–141
chewing, 18, 24
CKC (Canadian Kennel Club), 139
CKC (Continental Kennel Club), 139
clippers, nail trimming, 84

coats, 12, 61, 79–82, 86, 88
collars, training aid, 99–100
compulsion training, 99
costs, new puppy, 142–143
crates, 30–32, 100–102

Delta Society, therapy dogs, 105
diseases, vaccinations, 52–54
doggie dancing, 117–118
dog walkers, 32
dominance training, 98
dry (kibble) foods, 71–72

ears, 60–61, 84–85
England, Golden Retriever, 3–4
exercise, 107–118
ex-pens, training, 100–101
external parasites, 58–60
eyes, 47, 85–86

FCI (Federation Cynologique Internationale), 139
feet, 49, 83–84
females, 34, 36, 54–57, 122
flyball, 116, 118
foods, 49, 64–77
free-choice feeding, pros/cons, 74
Frisbee competition, 116, 118

genetic diseases, 46–49
Golden Retriever Clubs, 144
Golden Retriever rescue groups, 144
grass awns, 86
grooming, 7, 79–88
guarantees, health, 141

harness, training aid, 99–100
head halter, training aid, 100
health, 50–55, 64–70
health guarantees, 141
health organizations, 146
health problems, 46–50, 57–62, 66–70, 75, 85–88
heart, genetic diseases, 48

heatstroke, 61–62
hotspots, skin problem, 87
housebreaking, 35, 102–103
hunting dog clubs, 145

internal parasites, 57–58
Internet, breeder resource, 128–129
Irish Setter, 4

jogging, exercise opportunity, 114
jumping up, puppy behavior, 93

kidneys, chronic interstitial nephritis,
    69–70

labels, food information, 73–74
limited registration, AKC, 138
litter registration, 138

males, 34, 36, 54–57, 122
minerals, 65–66, 72–73

nail trimming, 83–84
Newfoundland, 4
newspaper ads, puppy source, 132
nutrition, 64–70, 73

obedience trials, 117
obesity, overfeeding risk, 75
OFA (Orthopedic Foundation for
    Animals), 141

pack mentality, 6–7, 18–19
parasites, internal/external, 57–60
pedigrees, 137–138, 140–141
PennHip, 141
physical development, 34–36, 108–111
puppies
    crate confinement, 101–102
    exercise requirements, 107–108
    feeding frequency, 68
    housebreaking, 35, 102–103
    jumping up behavior, 93
    new home, 121–122, 128
    nutritional requirements, 67–68
    pet versus show quality, 127

price ranges, 142–143
sick puppy avoidance, 133
slow maturing, 11
socialization requirements, 40–42
space requirements, 120
temperament testing, 17–19, 26–27
vaccinations, 52–54
purebred dog clubs, 144

questions
    breeder evaluation, 125–127
    new owner evaluation, 124–125

rakes, grooming aid, 80
registration
    AKC (American Kennel Club),
        137–138
    AKC statistics, 9–10
    ARBA (American Rare Breed Asso-
        ciation), 139
    authorities, 138–140
    CKC (Canadian Kennel Club), 139
    CKC (Continental Kennel Club),
        139
    FCI (Federation Cynologique Inter-
        nationale), 139
    limited, 138
    pedigrees, 137–138
    purpose of, 136
    UKC (United Kennel Club), 139
rescue kennels, 9, 11, 133–134
resources, 144–147
retriever tests/trials, 115–116
running lines, avoidance, 111–112
Russian Trackers, development, 3–4

semimoist foods, 71
senior dogs
    calluses, 61, 88
    developmental traits, 43–44
    exercise requirements, 109
    kidney impairment risk, 69–70
    nutritional requirements, 68–70
    rescue kennels, 133–134
separation anxiety, 31–32
service dogs, 104–105

service organizations, 147
shampoos, canine, 83
shedding, 6, 81
show quality, 127, 142
skin
    allergies, 49
    calluses, 61, 88
    genetic diseases, 47
    hotspots, 87
socialization, 18–19, 40–42
strangers, acceptance of, 23
stress, diet alteration, 66–67
supplements, foods, 72–73
swimming, exercise opportunity, 113

table scraps, food use, 77
teeth, cleaning, 87–88
temperament
    behavior versus, 25–26
    changing faulty, 28
    importance of, 26
    personality traits, 19–20
    predictability of, 27–28
    puppy testing, 26–27
    reason for abandonment, 28–29
therapy dogs, 105
thyroid gland, genetic diseases, 47
titles, pedigree element, 140–141
toes, nail trimming, 83–84
toothpaste, canine, 87–88
tracking trials, 115
trainability, 7, 90–91
training
    associative learning, 97–98
    CGC (Canine Good Citizen), 104
    class/club advantages, 94
    collar/leash guidelines, 99–100
    compulsion, 99
    crates, 100–102
    dominance, 98
    ex-pens, 100–101
    housebreaking, 35, 102–103
    importance of, 91–93
    mental development, 39
    owner's time requirements, 92
    paper-training, 103

principles, 94–97
professional help, 93–94
service dogs, 104–105
therapy dogs, 105
trainability, 90–91
treats, food types, 75–76
Tweed Water Spaniel, 4

UKC (United Kennel Club), registra-
    tion authority, 139
United States, breed introduction, 3

vaccinations, 52–54
veterinarians
    anal sac emptying, 88
    dental care, 88
    desirable traits, 52
    locating, 52
    spay/neuter services, 54–55, 57
    special diet source, 70
    vaccinations, 52–54
    yearly health costs, 50–51
vision, genetic diseases, 47
vitamins
    food supplements, 72–73
    nutritional element, 65–66

walking, exercise opportunity, 113
watchdogs, shortcoming, 6
weather (temperature)
    heatstroke concern, 61–62
    new dog considerations, 121–122
weight, description, 2, 35

X-rays, hip dysplasia determination,
    141

yards
    exercise opportunity, 108
    home-alone dogs, 30–32
yearly food costs, 73
yearly health costs, 50–51